VOLUME 91 • NUMI

NATIONAL

CIVIC

REVIEW

MAKING CITIZEN DEMOCRACY WORK

IN THIS ISSUE

New Directions in
Political Reform

Christopher T. Gates
President, National Civic League

Robert Loper
Editor

A Publication of the National Civic League and Jossey-Bass

NATIONAL CIVIC REVIEW (ISSN 0027-9013) is published quarterly by Wiley Subscription Services, Inc., A Wiley Company, at Jossey-Bass, 989 Market Street, San Francisco, CA 94103-1741, and the National Civic League, 1445 Market Street, Suite 300, Denver, CO 80202-1717. NCL, founded in 1894 as the National Municipal League, advocates a new civic agenda to create communities that work for everyone. NCL is a 501(c)(3) nonprofit, nonpartisan educational association of individuals and organizations. NCL members have access to the information and services necessary to improve community life. For complete information, contact Derek Okubo, (303) 571-4343.

INDEXED in Public Affairs Information Service, ABC POL SCI, and Book Review Index.

SUBSCRIPTIONS for individuals are $60 per year in the United States, Canada, and Mexico, and $84 per year in the rest of the world. Subscriptions for institutions are $115 in the United States, $155 in Canada and Mexico, and $189 in the rest of the world. To order subscriptions, single issues, or reprints, please refer to the Ordering Information page at the back of this issue.

PERIODICALS postage paid at San Francisco, California, and at additional mailing offices. POSTMASTER: send address changes to National Civic Review, Jossey-Bass Inc., 989 Market Street, San Francisco, CA 94103-1741.

NCL MEMBERS send change of address to Debbie Gettings, National Civic League, 1445 Market Street, Suite 300, Denver, CO 80202-1717.

EDITORIAL CORRESPONDENCE should be sent to Robert Loper, National Civic League, 1319 F Street NW, Suite 204, Washington, DC 20004.

www.josseybass.com

LETTERS TO THE EDITOR. *National Civic Review* welcomes letters to the editor. Write to *National Civic Review*, 1319 F Street, Suite 204, Washington, DC 20004, or send e-mail to robert@ncldc.org. Please include your name, address, and telephone number.

CONTENTS

NOTE FROM THE PRESIDENT   303
Christopher T. Gates

ARTICLES

The Politics of Reform in the Fifty-Fifty Nation   305
Mark Schmitt

The narrow division of the electorate between two major political
parties is the outcome of five interlocking elements of our political
system: the role of money in politics, the broadcast monopoly on
campaign communications, the low level of voter turnout, the effects
of redistricting on incumbency, and the superficial malleability of the
political issues put forth by the political parties. Political reform must
be directed at each of these five elements if we are to succeed in opening up our politics to new candidates, new ideas, and new voters.

Behind Closed Doors: The Recurring Plague of Redistricting   317
and the Politics of Geography
Steven Hill

In Election 2002, 98 percent of House incumbents seeking reelection
were returned to office. Only 39 of the 435 seats were competitively
contested, with a margin of victory of 10 points or less. In our single-
member-district, winner-take-all voting system, the decennial redistricting process can have a determinative influence on electoral
outcomes for years into the future.

Redistricting Reforms   331
Eric C. Olson

A number of states have established a means of safeguarding the public interest within the redistricting process. In addition to reviewing
the details of these procedures, this article raises the question of
whether a full-representation voting system should be part of such
reforms.

New Means for Political Empowerment in the Asian Pacific   335
American Community
Steven Hill, Robert Richie

Full-representation voting methods can increase the political representation of racial minorities above that which exists in the current
single-member district, winner-take-all system. Examples from
New York, San Francisco, and Los Angeles indicate how the Asian
Pacific American community might benefit from such voting methods.

Taking Democracy to Scale: Creating a Town Hall Meeting   351
for the Twenty-First Century
Carolyn J. Lukensmeyer, Steve Brigham

> Information technology can be used to make large-scale public delib-
> erations possible in a town hall setting. Through a sophisticated
> process design, citizens can deliberate together about major public
> issues and gain the attention of the news media and public decision
> makers. The recent Listening to the City event in New York City,
> which addressed rebuilding at Ground Zero, illustrates how this
> model can enhance citizens' voices in the democratic process.

The Vanishing Voter: Why Are the Voting Booths So Empty?   367
Thomas E. Patterson

> Voter turnout in presidential elections has been trending downward
> since 1960, with only 51 percent of the country casting a vote in
> 2000. Under the auspices of the Shorenstein Center at Harvard Uni-
> versity, the Vanishing Voter project interviewed nearly one hundred
> thousand voters during the 2000 election to uncover some of the rea-
> sons for this decline.

Healthy Municipalities: Now "It's the Only Way to Go!"   379
Leonard J. Duhl, M.D.

> This article, based on an address given at the Pan American Health
> Organization by one of the founders of the Healthy Cities/Healthy
> Communities movement, addresses the broad concept of community
> health in the Latin American context.

NOTE FROM THE PRESIDENT

Passage of the Bipartisan Campaign Reform Act (BCRA) was the most significant legislative reform of the federal campaign finance system in more than a quarter-century. However, while this achievement is indeed substantive, its ultimate impact remains unclear. Events that have occurred since the bill was signed into law illustrate the challenges that confront political reform efforts. The Federal Election Commission (FEC) has issued proposed regulations that would greatly limit the law's impact. Many incumbents in Congress, having successfully competed under the existing rules, do not have strong incentives to support comprehensive reform and therefore may not vocally oppose the FEC's clear weakening of the law. Furthermore, opponents of the new restrictions on soft money have brought suit in court, and the Supreme Court will ultimately rule on the constitutionality of the legislation.

Proponents of this round of legislative reform take the long view of the reform process, as well they should. Regardless of how the contests over BCRA are resolved, much more will remain to be done in the cause of political reform. No one ever believed that this legislation alone would or could completely reform our political process. However, with the recent ruling by the Second Circuit Court of Appeals that upheld Vermont's limits on campaign expenditures by state candidates, the legal straightjacket stitched by the Supreme Court in *Buckley* v. *Valeo* may be loosening. This should catalyze other efforts to pursue similar reforms. In this possibly more tolerant legal climate, states and local jurisdictions can play an important role in generating new reforms and providing the empirical record by which to assess the effects of those reforms. We do not know enough about what types of reform measures may be feasible, and one way to gauge this is to encourage experimentation on the part of states and local jurisdictions. Following Justice Brandeis's oft-quoted remarks, these laboratories may yield new approaches for realizing the essential end of limiting the influence of money in politics.

One of the things that NCL has learned through its New Politics program is that many citizens are not apathetic; rather, they lack a clear means for getting involved in politics in a way that matters to them. There is a growing level of activity around issues that are close to home, as the success of neighborhood watch programs attests. While engagement in traditional political activities remains lower than we would like, we believe that people become involved in issues they are concerned about when they think they can have an impact on them. We believe that one reason reform at the local level is so important is that it can help create a political climate that is supportive of reform at the state and federal levels as well.

Political reform is at the heart of NCL's mission, so we have once again devoted an issue of the *National Civic Review* to this topic. As noted in the article by Mark Schmitt, the electorate in this country is closely divided, notwithstanding the results of the 2002 election. Schmitt identifies the key characteristics of our closed and deadlocked political system and highlights opportunities for reformers to make some necessary changes. In an excerpt from his book *The Vanishing Voter,* Thomas E. Patterson analyzes the downturn in voter turnout and proposes remedies to reverse this trend. A set of articles by staff from the Center for Voting and Democracy focuses on the relationships among incumbency, redistricting, and electoral competitiveness in making a case for substantive voting system reform. Carolyn J. Lukensmeyer and Steve Brigham, from America*Speaks,* note the difficulties in conducting town hall deliberations in the modern age and detail the facilitated dialogue they conducted among nearly five thousand New Yorkers about the future of Ground Zero. This deliberative model provides a technologically sophisticated means for renewing the democratic form of the town hall meeting.

It is a personal pleasure to publish the remarks of Leonard J. Duhl, M.D., one of the founders of the Healthy Cities/Healthy Communities movement, with which NCL has long been associated. Duhl's address on community was delivered at a ceremony at the Pan American Health Organization, where he received the Abraham Horvitz Award in recognition of his important contributions to improving health in the Americas. We think his remarks and the ideas in these articles will provide inspiration and insight to the political reform community at large as we collectively take up the continuing work of improving our democracy.

CHRISTOPHER T. GATES
PRESIDENT, NATIONAL CIVIC LEAGUE

The Politics of Reform in the Fifty-Fifty Nation

Mark Schmitt

During the last weeks of the 2002 congressional elections, a concept familiar to political scientists suddenly became part of the conventional wisdom: the idea of the fifty-fifty nation, with an electorate divided almost evenly between the two major parties, in which elections are decided by the marginal voter at the 50 percent line. This was more than just a description of current circumstances, and it began to seem that this situation was likely to persist and even to reinforce itself, and that perhaps it was an inevitable result of the current practice of politics.

The idea first emerged in the 2000 election, which was actually as close to a fifty-fifty election as possible, with the electoral vote for president coming down to a handful of questionable ballots in one state, and the Senate exactly divided. (The popular vote for president and the makeup of the House of Representatives both produced more decisive results, but not for the same party.) The 2002 election ended with a gentle but decisive swing toward the Republicans, shattering Democratic expectations of gains, but in a sense it proved the point: a tiny shift in public opinion can produce a huge effect on the actual configuration of power. The underlying result was still very much in equipoise: one elected incumbent senator from each party was defeated, and (excluding elections that pitted two incumbents against each other) just two Democratic House incumbents and two Republican House incumbents lost reelection. Democrats lost a total of two seats in the Senate and two in the House. This was one of the smallest shifts ever, especially after redistricting. Governorships are now split at twenty-five for each party. Several state legislatures are also divided, or control was decided by a few party-switchers, and the aggregate national balance of state legislators is also evenly split. The fifty-fifty nation is alive, if not well.

An evenly divided electorate may just be a fact of life. There's nothing inherently preferable about a fifty-five to forty-five electorate, or a seventy-thirty electorate! But the evidence suggests that there is something different about the current division. It seems to be self-reinforcing and driven by factors other than the natural ideological split among American voters. It is also unhealthy. Several factors in recent politics seem to reinforce this unstable equilibrium. It is these factors that should set a broader agenda of reform for U.S. democracy:

- *Money in politics.* Centrally controlled by the political parties, and virtually unavailable to most challengers until they are deemed to have a good shot at winning, money has much to do with the stasis of the fifty-fifty nation.
- *The broadcast monopoly over campaign communications.* Although they have been granted a public trust to use a currently scarce common resource—the broadcast spectrum—radio and television broadcasters reap huge profits by assuming the role of gatekeeper over most of the communications between candidates and voters.
- *A limited electorate.* Both parties assume that the population of voters will not change dramatically, and they are generally not eager to deal with the unpredictability that would ensue if it did. They invest little effort in broadening the electorate; in many cases, they strive to limit it. That Democrats as well as Republicans would prefer the voting population to remain basically as it is can be shown by California governor Gray Davis's opposition to an initiative to allow would-be voters to register on election day, which was defeated.
- *Incumbent protection in redistricting.* It is unprecedented that the first congressional election after a redistricting cycle, as this was, should produce so little turnover. But redistricting has become so partisan, the techniques so sophisticated, and the natural compromise in closely divided state legislatures so likely to involve protecting all incumbents, that only about forty congressional races were competitive, and a good number of those were in states where a population decrease had forced two incumbents to face each other.
- *Superficially malleable issue positions.* On one level, the two parties have never been further apart on their basic approach to issues, particularly economics. But on the face of it, they have never seemed closer together. Thirty-seven percent of voters in 2002 said they thought the parties' positions on most issues were more or less identical. Imagine what nonvoters thought! When either party seems to gain an edge on a popular issue, the other, aided by the rapid response capacity of the modern media, moves quickly to match it. Democrats sought to match Republicans on homeland security, military action in Iraq, and tax cuts. Republicans countered Democratic advantages on prescription drug coverage for seniors, and especially on Social Security privatization. If the parties were truly malleable—that is, responding and changing on the basis of the public's views—this would hardly be a problem and might represent responsive democracy at its healthiest. But instead, the parties' malleable faces disguise fairly rigid and divergent positions. For example, after insisting in the election campaign that they had no intention of privatizing Social Security, and demanding that the press not use the word, days after the election the president and other leading Republicans declared it a mandate for their Social Security plans. (Since Democrats did not take power, it is not

possible to find an exact parallel, but in the interest of balance, note that most Democrats argued that there was no policy difference between their party and the White House on the question of military confrontation with Iraq; yet it is indubitable that had any Democrat held the White House, the course of events would not have followed the same path.)

It is these five pillars, and not merely a natural ideological division, on which the existence and self-perpetuation of the fifty-fifty nation rests. These pillars reinforce one another, locking politics into a degrading and diminishing cycle in which the fullest possibilities of democracy go unrealized. For example, the broadcast monopoly on political communication exacerbates the pressure on money and the exclusion of candidates who can't raise it. The malleability of candidates' claimed positions on issues encourages voters to think there are no major differences between the parties, which deepens the cynicism that discourages full participation. The limited electorate, in turn, increases the relative payoff to strongly negative advertising, which in turn requires an advantage in broadcast time and thus money. The paucity of competitive seats, because of redistricting, allows the parties to concentrate resources on just a few, and the campaign then becomes a showdown between outside financial resources rather than the candidates themselves. And so it goes.

Further, these forces lead to a concentration of political attention on that marginal voter at the fiftieth percentile, who has some real possibility of switching votes or staying home. The concerns of millions of voters who are taken for granted either as loyal voters to one party or another or as nonvoters go virtually unheard in the election process. For this reason, politics focuses on issues such as the patient's bill of rights, protecting those who have health coverage through HMOs, rather than the forty-one million people without health insurance at all.

It is therefore no surprise that, as the *Washington Post* noted in a news article shortly before the election, each year party leaders and advisers pledge to seek out big ideas and radical realignments, yet each election year they fall back to a predictable campaign along familiar negative lines and appealing to the marginal voter. These forces form a vicious circle; the challenge for advocates of a more invigorated democracy is to break the cycle, turning one or two of these forces around. This alone might be enough to create a virtuous circle, in which the strengths of American democracy reassert themselves and reinforce others, as they have done so many times in the past.

We are facing a great confrontation in American politics. It is not between Democrats and Republicans, or liberals and conservatives. Nor is it between some ideal of "clean" politics and a corrupt system, because no political system is free of the temptation of private interests. Rather it is a confrontation between the closed politics of the fifty-fifty nation and an open politics in which there is more opportunity for new candidates, new ideas, new voters, and new majorities to emerge, shift, and realign. The closed politics of the perpetual fifty-fifty nation is the combined symptom when all the antidemocratic forces in our politics come together.

The goal of a political reform agenda should be to address each of the self-perpetuating causes of the fifty-fifty nation and dismantle them one by one. The first cause is the role of money in politics. Reformers have often focused principally on direct corruption, the implicit corruption of large contributions, or the unequal access and power of large contributors. All these concerns are important. But the goal of opening the system must also be a part of the agenda for campaign finance reformers. In the last several years there have been major breakthroughs in campaign finance reform, at both the federal and state levels, many of which will open the system and others that may not. I consider these in more detail below.

Second, as Senators John McCain and Russell Feingold affirmed after their astonishing victory on campaign finance reform, the next step is to address the cost of political communication, not just the sources of money, by reestablishing that broadcasters bear a public responsibility that stems from their public grant to use the airwaves for profit. A broadcast time bank, as described by Matt Farrey in an earlier issue of this journal (*NCR* volume 90, issue 2), would create one forum through which candidates could communicate their ideas free of the pressures of money.

Third, we must open up the electorate. This means making it easier to vote, removing artificial barriers to voting, and encouraging the political parties—through campaign finance regulation and other forces—to make every effort to draw new voters to the polls rather than fight a zero-sum game within the existing electorate. Campaigns face a choice with each ad and mailing they put out: they can try to convert a voter who leans against them to switch, which is very difficult. Or they can try to get a truly neutral voter or nonvoter to turn out and vote for their candidate, which takes a lot of effort in the current system. There is a third choice: they can try to persuade a voter who supports the other side to stay home, through negative ads. This third choice is often the most tempting and the least risky. Reform efforts must change this self-perpetuating calculus.

Allowing voters to register on the day of the election would be one way to change the calculus. If campaigns had less certainty about just who could vote, they would look at the calculation differently, making more effort to reach those unknown voters. Same-day voter registration quite plainly lends a level of uncertainty to elections that is a healthy challenge to all candidates, as former Minnesota Governor Jesse Ventura proved. Further, we have to ask, if voting is "the most important right" held by Americans—as the naturalization test for new citizens puts it—why is it the only right that, to be exercised, requires us to register weeks in advance?

The fourth piece of the agenda is to address redistricting. It's always too early to address redistricting (the next census is eight years away), and then it's too late. The time is now, when sitting elected officials are not yet worrying about the 2012 election, to put in place some reasonable criteria that will produce districts that are not designed entirely to protect incumbents. Iowa's experience with a nonpartisan commission that created four of the forty competitive House districts in the country is an obvious example of the way to go, although Iowa is Iowa and redistricting is a jealously guarded prerogative of almost every legislature.

Progress in making these changes should have a significant impact on the fifth pillar, the superficial malleability of the positions the two parties take on many issues. A more open politics with new ideas and new players—both candidates and voters—should produce greater clarity in expressing substantive policy positions and the differences between the parties.

A Case Study in the Fight for Open Politics: Campaign Finance Reform

Passage in 2002 of the Shays-Meehan and McCain-Feingold legislation banning soft money and making other changes to campaign finance law was the first significant victory in the long struggle to open politics, and also the most remarkable legislative accomplishment since the Tax Reform Act of 1987. To pass Shays-Meehan, supporters had to overcome every procedural assumption of politics-as-usual: that House members never defy their leadership by signing a discharge petition (they did), that the Senate never passes House bills unchanged (it did), that coalitions never stick together through every amendment (the reform coalition in the House did), and that senators never influence House members (John McCain did).

The accomplishment is all the more remarkable when one considers that, aside from a hard core of passionate reformers identified with the issue, almost every member of Congress would have been just as happy to see the bill die, because every one of them has at least mastered the current rules and has reason to fear any change. Further, the bill passed even though—on nationwide polls, and despite the Enron scandal—campaign finance reform still barely registers in the single digits among issues that matter to voters. Perhaps most remarkably, the bill was not significantly watered down along its path to passage. Although a useful amendment from the bill that passed the Senate in 2001, which would have reduced television costs, was dropped, the overall bill went further than the version that Senators McCain and Feingold introduced in 1999.

The Legislation and Its Limits. For all that it represents as an achievement, the legislation itself is assuredly not, as the *New York Times* wishfully called it, a "sweeping overhaul" of the system by which campaigns are financed. Even its sponsors did not make that claim. It closes one major loophole, through which long-prohibited corporate and labor union money, in unlimited and staggering amounts, came directly to influence the outcomes of federal elections. That loophole was soft money. Without soft money, corporate money will no longer directly fund campaigns or parties; and million-dollar contributions, though not expelled from politics, will at least have some distance from campaigns and elected officials. Once again, as was the case from 1976 through the early 1990s, only individuals will contribute to candidates and parties, and only in limited amounts. Further, independent committees will not be allowed to run ads obviously intended to influence an election within sixty days before a general election or thirty days before a primary, unless they follow all the rules on disclosure that apply to other independent expenditures. Finally, certain changes are intended to increase the supply of hard money—that is, limited money from individuals. The limit on a single contribution to a federal candidate is raised to $2,000 from $1,000, the aggregate total that a person can give to all candidates and parties is increased, and a new category is created for limited contributions to state and local parties for voter registration and turnout efforts.

These are essential reforms, long overdue, and there is no doubt that when they take effect they will discombobulate the routines, rituals, and tricks that political operatives have mastered over the years. But after the disruption, what comes next? Is it a dramatically improved situation, in which money matters less than ideas, as Senate Majority Leader Tom Daschle put it? Is it the same big-money game in a different form? Or is it a different set of problems, requiring new solutions? The remainder of this article looks at these questions, and at the areas that activists and funders who recognize the work still to be done on the issue of money in politics should be watching.

In the days after the House passed Shays-Meehan, making its ultimate success inevitable, the opinion pages filled with earnest predictions about exactly what could be expected. Yet paradoxical results occur frequently in the world of campaign finance. Each of the predictions, from supporters as well as opponents, should be treated as an area for scrutiny, for ongoing research.

In the vast zone between McCain-Feingold and the as-yet-unimagined legislation that will finally strike the proper balance between money and democracy, there are three issues that merit close attention.

Hard Money. Most attention, and criticism, has been given to the possible effect of the increase in the hard money contribution limit to $2,000. Although this increase was a compromise necessary to get the bill passed, the new limit is not as high as the $3,000 that many foresaw as the logical update of the 1974 limit of $1,000 into current dollars. But opponents on the left worry that it will further concentrate political influence in the hands of the tiny fraction of the population that is wealthy enough to give any significant amount to a political campaign.

Looking at this issue in terms of open politics, however, would call for greater attention to its effect on the supply of political money and the competitiveness of races. Of more concern than the influence of $2,000 donors should be the fact that it's now virtually impossible to become a competitive candidate for the House or the Senate while raising money entirely in $1,000 contributions. The price of entry into a competitive race for the House now starts at $1 million. With a single exception, every House freshman elected in a reasonably competitive district in 2000 spent at least $1 million. (The exception, by the way, spent $915,000.)

Nevertheless, only eighty nonincumbent candidates (both challengers and open-seat candidates) in 2000 had a million dollars to spend. Of that eighty, one-third financed their campaigns mostly with their own money, leaving just fifty-four nonincumbents who reached the threshold for competitiveness through hard money alone, even including political action committee contributions. This fact, even more than the potential corruption of larger contributions, is the problem of money in politics. It is not the problem of too much money, but that too few candidates have enough of it.

In this light, the higher contribution limit should be seen as an open question. Is it possible that the higher limit will help challengers who now cannot be heard to reach the threshold? Yes, it's possible. Every plausible candidate probably begins with a core of two hundred or three hundred old friends, classmates, professional acquaintances, and well-off local activists. If those allies can each give $2,000 instead of just $1,000, then the candidate might have a better chance of reaching the million dollars needed. Of the few people who can give $1,000, most can also give $2,000 without a noticeably greater corrupting influence.

On the other hand, because individual donors still give more to incumbents than to challengers, the $2,000 limit could mean that incumbents can put themselves further out of reach than ever. The price of entering a congressional race could reach $2 million, or it could be that challengers will get closer to the threshold of viability but most will still fall short. My own guess is that this last outcome is more likely, but we should all keep an open and observant mind.

Self-Financed Candidates. Given that it's all but impossible to run for office on hard money alone, superwealthy candidates who can fund their own campaigns have become a central feature of the political system. Self-financed candidates have always been with us, and they are often dismissed as relatively harmless, because so many, blessed with more ego than political sense, flame out spectacularly. But in recent years, self-financed candidates have become a systemic element of the political process, especially for Democrats. Consider this: Democrats control the Senate because of wealthy candidates. Exactly half of the Democratic senators who defeated Republican incumbents over the last two elections financed their own campaigns. For nonincumbent Senate candidates, the largest source of funds was the candidates themselves, not individuals, political action committees, or parties.

The self-financed Democrats of most recent vintage—Senators John Edwards, Jon Corzine, Mark Dayton, and Maria Cantwell—have shown themselves to be as capable, liberal, and brave as their older counterparts such as John D. Rockefeller IV. Corzine's knowledgeable leadership on 401(k) retirement plan reform, in the wake of the Enron scandal, is just one example of these legislators' independence. But there is no getting around the fact that the advantage of self-financed candidates has created a political plutocracy that looks less like America, economically, than at any time since before direct election of senators. More than one hundred members of Congress are now millionaires. Yet many reformers seem more concerned about the power of wealthy individuals when they donate to others than when they win office themselves.

Without soft money, the number and advantage of self-financers is likely to increase. One can see this just by looking at the recruitment patterns of the Democratic Senate Campaign Committee. In each state, the DSCC looked first for a very popular statewide elected official, such as Governors Tom Carper of Delaware and Mel Carnahan of Missouri. Absent that, they looked for candidates who could fund their own campaign. A third option was to take less well-known challengers, such as Debbie Stabenow of Michigan, and infuse their campaign with soft money. Without the third option, the party will face even more pressure to find the second. Republicans have a deeper base of hard-money contributors, so they do not face so stark a choice.

The McCain-Feingold bill actually includes a provision intended to offset the advantage of self-financers, but it takes exactly the wrong approach. It allows candidates facing a wealthy opponent to accept contributions of up to $6,000 and to ignore limits on spending coordinated with the party. This is surely the most offensive provision in the bill. If $2,000 contribution limits are fair for challengers facing well-known and well-funded incumbents, why are they too low for incumbents facing wealthy challengers? One can only hope that this exception meets with a vigorous challenge to its constitutionality. There are far better ways to offset the advantage of self-financed candidates and help ordinary challengers as well as incumbents.

Outside Money. Soft money through political parties was never the only way that million-dollar gifts, and corporate or union money, entered political campaigns. Independent committees registered under Section 527 of the tax code could serve virtually the same purpose as parties, and even 501(c)(4) nonprofits can run ads that might influence elections. The legislation will significantly shrink this loophole. By prohibiting elected officials from raising money for such committees, it will eliminate the politicians' committees that a large number of members of Congress had established as a way to accept and use large or corporate contributions. (Representative Tom DeLay, a leading reform opponent, had several.) By prohibiting television ads that mention a candidate in the period leading up to the election, it will shut down the most effective way for these committees to be used to influence elections.

These provisions will be challenged in court. They are well drafted to withstand constitutional challenge, but in the event that they are overturned, then McCain-Feingold might as well have not passed at all.[1] The soft money now moving through political parties will instead be used to fund 527s, which will run the same thinly disguised ads currently being run by parties.

But even if these provisions stand, it is likely that the activity of independent committees will increase, as corporations, labor unions, and advocacy groups seek ways to retain their political influence. For one thing, plenty of very effective campaign ads are aired months before an election, often in an effort to demolish an opponent's reputation before he or she has a chance to start running ads. (Bob Dole's 1996 presidential candidacy never recovered from the Democrats' soft-money ad barrage of late 1995.) There are also effective ads that don't mention a candidate at all. Do they really need to? Wouldn't an ad touting tax cuts benefit a Republican? Or an ad promoting prescription drug coverage benefit a Democrat, especially if it echoed a candidate's themes? Former California governor Pete Wilson devised the technique of creating a big-money slush fund by running a campaign on a ballot initiative on a popular issue such as crime side-by-side with a campaign for office on the same themes.

Although many operatives still believe that an ad that doesn't name a candidate is ineffective, they are beginning to see that there are other options. In 2000, for example, pro-choice groups ran an aggressive campaign, targeted toward pro-choice Republican and independent women in a handful of swing states. The ads did little more than remind women that abortion rights were at risk and that the next president would appoint the justices who would determine whether *Roe v. Wade* survives, on the basis of research showing that women were complacent about reproductive rights. They did not win the electoral college for Vice President Gore, but these ads probably helped him win several targeted states in the Midwest.

There's nothing wrong with such ads, and they belong in a vibrant, pluralist democracy in which interest groups, candidates, and parties compete for voters' attention. The shift of money from parties toward groups with distinct issue viewpoints, and toward communications that highlight issues rather than attack candidates, could be a healthy development. A politics of issues and not personality should be something that all of us good-government types would applaud.

But there's another version of the same issue ad that's far less benign, in which corporate interests hide behind issue groups in an effort to influence elections. The *Los Angeles Times* recently revealed that Enron lobbyist Ed Gillespie, a longtime aide to House GOP leader Dick Armey, had devised a plan to use ads discussing the Bush administration's energy plan as "a political weapon against Democrats." The ads, some of which depicted Jimmy Carter in a reminder of the energy crises of the 1970s, were sponsored by a new group called the "21st Century Energy Project," with Gillespie as its director and funding undisclosed.

This is the future. It will be far easier to convert corporate and union money now contributed to the parties as soft money into this kind of soft issue ad than to convert it into hard money.

There is another danger to substituting either corporate or interest group issue ads for party soft money. It is the risk that, with limits placed on both candidates and parties but outside groups unrestricted, the voice of outside groups will come to dominate and shape the agenda of a campaign. At worst, candidates will become bystanders to their own campaigns. In Wisconsin, as Alan Ehrenhalt reported in the magazine *Governing* in 2000, campaigns are already dominated by two broad clusters of interest groups, one led by the teachers' union and the other by the state's business and industry association, which sometimes outspend both candidates in key races. Candidates wake up in the morning to radio ads attacking or praising them, ads that they neither wrote nor approved. One lobbyist told Ehrenhalt, "It's interesting that the candidates seem to think the campaigns belong to them."

The Limits of Limits

Perhaps some of the potential problems discussed here will not emerge, or will take a different form. But they all have one thing in common: they cannot be solved by further *limits* on political money. Limits will not help challengers or new voices be heard. Limits on candidates' spending on their own campaigns, or on interest groups' right to speak on their issues, will not survive constitutional scrutiny. Nor should they.

McCain-Feingold, then, is not the last word on campaign finance reform. But it should be the last bill of its kind—the last that has as its goal "getting money out of politics." The next step in campaign finance reform must involve making it easier for candidates to be heard, and increasing competition. It should give candidates, including incumbents, new ways to fund their campaigns without having to pursue special-interest donors relentlessly, press the edge of the envelope on outside money, or use their own wealth. It must involve public financing, ideally in combination with free television time for candidates, because it is the price of television advertising that has made a million dollars the price of entry.

Public financing can take several forms, and each is likely to have merits and drawbacks, some as yet unknown:

• New York City's system provides a public match of $4 for every $1 in contributions of less than $250. In 2001, this approach created vibrant city council races with six or seven viable candidates in some districts. Although Mayor Michael Bloomberg has been accused of "trashing" the system by financing his own campaign, keep in mind that the system allowed Democrat Mark Green to spend $17 million in combined public and private funds—an amount that only a handful of candidates in U.S. history have ever had available, and probably enough for his message to be heard.

• Maine and Arizona this year completed their second election cycles under a system known as "clean money," which provides full funding of a campaign at a fixed amount for candidates who agree to take no private money beyond small qualifying contributions to show broad support. A recent study of these systems in their first run showed that they were attractive to candidates of both parties, and that they brought in candidates who otherwise would not have been able to run or who hated fundraising. In Arizona this year, 70 percent of legislative candidates participated, along with all but one of the candidates for governor. The system is popular with voters; Senator McCain, who as a candidate in the 2000 presidential primaries opposed public financing, has become an enthusiastic supporter.

• A third approach to public financing is the tax credit. Minnesota, for example, offers a full, refundable tax credit for any political contribution of up to $50. This is combined with a one-to-one match, so every citizen, in effect, gets a free $100 to make his or her political voice heard. This is a good way to encourage politicians to seek smaller contributors as well as a way to help candidates be heard.

Insiders will debate the relative merits of these approaches endlessly. But we must not become mired in the technicalities. The key questions are not whether these programs eliminate all private money or the potential for corruption, but whether they open up politics to new ideas, new candidates, new voices, and a broader electorate. If they can, they may be the first step in dismantling all the pillars that hold up the fifty-fifty nation and keep us from realizing our full potential as a twenty-first-century democracy.

Note

1. The *San Francisco Chronicle* recently noted the kind of ad that could lead to the provision being overturned: a radio ad in Illinois urging House Speaker Dennis Hastert to bring legislation banning employment discrimination against gays and lesbians to the House floor. The ad was funded by the ACLU. The ad mentioned Hastert and happened to run right before the Illinois primary in which his name was on the ballot, but it was not intended to influence the election. Such ads are rare, but just a few of them would bolster an argument that the provision is overly broad.

Mark Schmitt is director of the Program on Governance and Public Policy of the Open Society Institute.

Behind Closed Doors: The Recurring Plague of Redistricting and the Politics of Geography

Steven Hill

> We are in the business of rigging elections.
>
> —State Senator Mark McDaniel, _North Carolina_[1]

Beginning in early 2001, a great tragedy occurred in American politics. It happened quietly, for the most part behind closed doors, and with minimal public input or oversight. The net result of this tragedy is that most voters had their vote rendered nearly meaningless, almost as if it had been stolen from them. Yet the stealing happened without faulty voting equipment, poorly designed ballots, misused voter lists, or campaign finance abuses. It was more like a silent burglar in the middle of the night having his way while American voters slept. As a result of this theft, hallowed notions such as "no taxation without representation" and "one person, one vote" have been drained of their vitality, reduced to empty slogans for armchair patriots.

And it was all legal.

Not only was it legal, but the two major political parties, their incumbents, and their consultants were participants in the heist. Most political scientists, pundits, and journalists raised barely a peep, considering it to be standard operating procedure, part of the everyday give-and-take (mostly take) of America's winner-take-all politics. It's just how the game is played, apparently.

I'm referring to what is known as the process of redistricting, the decennial redrawing of legislative district lines. Following the 2000 Census, every legislative district in the United States—every city council district, every state legislative and

_This article has been adapted, with permission of the publisher, from the author's book _Fixing Elections: The Failure of America's Winner-Take-All Politics_ (New York: Routledge, 2002). More information about the issues discussed in this article can be found at www.FixingElections.com._

NATIONAL CIVIC REVIEW, vol. 91, no. 4, Winter 2002   © Wiley Periodicals, Inc.   317

U.S. House district, literally thousands and thousands of districts—had to be redrawn before the next elections in 2002 because by law these districts must all be roughly equal in population.

This line-drawing is the defining skirmish of the geographic-based, winner-take-all, single-seat district system. Newt Gingrich once said, "Redistricting is everything," and here's why: *the line-drawing decides—in advance—the winners and losers of most legislative elections for the next ten years.*

Guess who is redrawing the lines? Contrary to all sense—except the type of sense that has been steeped in defense of the status quo—the lines are usually redrawn by none other than the politicians themselves. These incumbent line-drawers generally are guided by no criteria other than two rather ambitious and self-serving goals: first, to guarantee their own reelection and that of their friends and colleagues; and second, to garner a majority of legislative seats for their political party or faction. When it comes to redistricting, the fox not only guards the hen house; the fox *salivates.*

The 2001–02 redistricting plans in most states amounted to little better than an incumbent protection plan, producing even fewer competitive districts than past efforts. In fact, as we will see, the 2001 redistricting was perhaps the most flagrantly rigged insider's racket in decades. Most voters were reduced to spectator status, their votes drained of vitality, as they were packed into partisan districts designed to guarantee the reelection of incumbents and the dominant party.

The Incumbent Protection Racket

> Every individual who participated in the redistricting process knew that incumbency protection was a critical factor in producing the bizarre lines. . . . Many of the oddest twists and turns of the Texas districts would never have been created if the Legislature had not been so intent on protecting party and incumbents.
>
> —U.S. Supreme Court Justice John Paul Stevens, *Bush v. Vera,*
> June 13, 1996

Forget what you've heard about Big Money buying elections. The rigging of winner-take-all, single-seat districts is the political class's slickest sleight of hand, and it descends upon us once a decade like a giant iceberg. Behind closed doors, party leaders and incumbents conduct the decennial ritual of carving up the political map as if it's their very own birthday cake. To accomplish their narrow goals, they jigsaw, jury-rig, and gerrymander[2] legislative districts, with little or no regulation or public oversight. They produce bizarrely contorted legislative districts that one party leader called "my contribution to modern art,"[3] with shapes resembling, in the words of a number of observers, splattered spaghetti sauce, a squashed mosquito, a meandering snake, dumbbells, earmuffs, a starfish, a gnawed wishbone, Bullwinkle the Moose, the "Z" mark of Zorro, and a host of other bewildering forms that defy description or explanation other than the capricious act of a powerful class of politicians looking to guarantee themselves lifetime employment and party preeminence.[4]

While the public mostly ignores redistricting, politicians know in the marrow of their bones how much redistricting matters. Previous redistricting episodes have been marked by physical violence and nearly fatal tragedies.[5] The 2001 redistricting in California, which was dominated by the Democratic Party, raised the incumbent protection plan to a crass new level. According to Representative Loretta Sanchez, she and thirty of the thirty-two Democratic U.S. House incumbents forked over $20,000 each to powerful consultant Michael Berman (brother of one of the Democratic incumbents), who was overseeing the line-drawing, to gerrymander for them a personal fiefdom in which they could not lose. To hear Sanchez talk about it, the money was tantamount to a bribe, the type of protection money one might pay to a local mafia don to protect your turf. "Twenty thousand is nothing to keep your seat," said Sanchez. "I spend $2 million [campaigning] every election."[6] This is practically the functional equivalent of insider trading by members of a powerful political class taking advantage of the rules to feather their own nest.

If the curtain was pulled back on the redistricting wizards, what the public would see are some of the most unflattering moments of our winner-take-all ritual. The process goes on behind closed doors, with technocrats hunched over computer screens remapping the most fundamental terrain of our democracy: the single-seat district. Depending on who is doing the line-drawing, most Democratic districts are carefully packed with enough registered Democratic voters, and Republican districts with enough Republican voters, to make it virtually impossible for anyone else to win except the favored incumbent or party. The last thing on politicians' minds is the impact of redistricting on the public, on voters, on the health of our republic, or on national policy. Redistricting single-seat districts thus is a direct threat to such key democratic values as electoral competition, representation, governance, and choice for voters.

Choiceless Elections: Watching Your Vote Disappear

> First they gerrymander us into one-party fiefs. Then they tell us they only care about the swing districts. Then they complain about voter apathy.
>
> —Gail Collins, *New York Times* columnist

Research has demonstrated that, as a result of single-seat districts and the accompanying redistricting roulette—and *not* inequities in campaign finances—the vast majority of U.S. House races are so noncompetitive as to be a done deal before voters even show up at the polls. To be precise, in the 2002 House elections 91 percent of races were won by a comfortable victory margin greater than ten points, and 83 percent were won by a landslide margin greater than twenty points (both of these figures include the seventy-six races that were uncontested by a major party). Only thirty-nine seats—a mere 9 percent of all House seats—were won by a competitive margin of fewer than ten points, the lowest figure in many years. Like a Soviet-type Politburo, 98 percent of incumbents won reelection, and most legislative elections were reduced to a meaningless charade.[7]

In fact, the 2001–02 congressional redistricting made an already egregious situation even worse. Typically, after redistricting there are more than 100 House seats up for grabs. After the 1991–92 redistricting, for instance, there were 121 competitive seats. But in 2002 there were fewer than 40. Of those 40, only half were really a toss-up, and that number will likely decrease as the decade progresses. By 2010 there will perhaps be a mere 15 or so races out of 435 where it will matter whether the voters show up at the polls or not. Redistricting—gerrymandering partisan districts—has become a glorified incumbent-protection racket that has robbed most voters of any semblance of choice or a competitive election.

State legislative elections generally were even worse. Astoundingly, of the thousands of state legislative races in 2002, 37 percent were *uncontested* by a major party (the figure was even higher in 1998 and 2000, when 41 percent of seats were uncontested by one of the two major parties).[8] Because the districts generally are so lopsided, it's a waste of campaign resources for the minority party to contest these seats. That's nearly two in five races in which the only choice for voters was to ratify the candidate of the dominant party, cast a hopeless vote for a third-party candidate, or not vote at all.

In fact, in Election 2002 sixteen states had all of their U.S. House seats either uncontested or won by a landslide; eleven more states had all but one of their U.S. House seats either uncontested or won by a landslide. Even the largest states were vastly uncompetitive, with California having fifty out of fifty-three of the U.S. House seats uncontested or won by a landslide, Florida having twenty-three out of twenty-five, New York having twenty-six out of twenty-nine, Texas having twenty-four out of thirty-two seats, Ohio having fifteen out of eighteen, Illinois having seventeen out of nineteen, Pennsylvania having fourteen out of nineteen, Michigan having thirteen out of fifteen, and Virginia having a perfect eleven out of eleven U.S. House seats uncontested or won by a landslide. That is an average of 87 percent in these nine large states, which collectively elect more than half of all U.S. House seats.

In other words, in 2002 there was not a lot of competition and not much viable choice for voters in the vast number of legislative races across the country, not even in our largest states. Moreover, not only is it true that the winner takes all in our system, but usually the winner takes all without even much of a fight. The average margin of victory in 2002 House races was 42 percent. Most races are so predictable that the Center for Voting and Democracy (CVD), like a handicapper at the racetrack, has been able to forecast the winners and the margin of victory in three-quarters of the U.S. House races months in advance with stunning accuracy. We do this without knowing anything about inequities in campaign finance or candidate strategy. CVD's technique is simply to estimate the partisan demographics of how the districts were gerrymandered during the last redistricting and how incumbents have fared in the district. CVD's predictions were 100 percent accurate for the 2002 elections, and 99.8 percent accurate for the previous three election cycles. Already we have predicted the winners for 2004—yes, that's right, 2004, nearly two years away—in more than 350 races. The overt partisanship of most legislative districts is so obvious that this has become a relatively easy exercise.[9]

With 90 percent of House races being a done deal before voters walk into the voting booth, this translates into an uninspiring campaign, if there is a campaign at all. The noncompetitive nature of most of these legislative races in the November elections is not due to inequity in campaign spending, as many analysts have assumed. Instead, it is due to the natural partisan demographics of where people live, combined with incumbent name recognition, and filtered through our geographic-based, winner-take-all system and its grotesquely gerrymandered districts. Campaign finance inequity matters more in party primaries for open seats and in close races, but open seats in federal races and states without term limits, as well as close races at any level, are few and far between. We like to think of our winner-take-all system as at least a two-party, two-choice affair, but in fact the frame of reference for most voters in most elections is that of a one-party system—the party that dominates their district.

Past redistricting has never been a model of fairness or exclamation of high democratic values, but this time around at least one new factor raised the stakes beyond anything previously experienced. Just as computers have had an impact on so many other areas of modern life, new computer technologies have dramatically altered the redistricting game. The politicians and their consultants now have at their disposal extremely sophisticated computer hardware and software, combined with the latest census, demographic, and polling data, to precisely gerrymander the political map. The days of plastic Mylar maps, magic markers, Elmer's glue, trial-and-error jigsaws, and cut-and-paste blueprints are over.

In fact, one can make a credible argument that, from now on, we will no longer choose our representatives; instead, the politicians will *choose us*. Every ten years, when the district lines are redrawn, winners and losers will be decided for most legislative districts and that will entrench the dominant party and incumbents for the rest of the decade. The lone choice of voters then will be simply to ratify the candidate from the dominant party awarded that district by the redistricting politicians some years before. From the voter's point of view, the candidate selection process, already an abject failure, has now become much worse. Henceforth the political game will be played much differently than ever before, and these new redistricting technologies are crucial to the new paradigm.

What role is the stark lack of choice playing in our abysmal voter turnout, which in 2002 saw a mere 39 percent of eligible adults going to the polls? Here is one indication: research has shown a strong correlation between voter turnout and competitiveness. For instance two separate studies by the Center for Voting and Democracy of 1994 U.S. House elections and 2000 U.S. House elections showed that voter turnout dropped dramatically by as much as nineteen points as House races became less competitive.[10] In the 2000 presidential election and 2002 congressional elections, voter turnout was highest in the key battleground states where the race was closest.[11]

Monopoly Politics, Political Monocultures, and the Loss of Political Ideas

> This new [redistricting] plan basically does away with the need for elections.
>
> —Tony Quinn, GOP redistricting consultant in California

Beyond what is happening to individual districts, redistricting is contributing to tens of millions of voters living in one-party *states*. The cumulative effect is to produce an entrenched political monoculture that is leading to an astonishing loss of political debate and ideas. For example, the 2002 U.S. House elections saw Massachusetts electing Democrats to all ten of its seats, and Nebraska electing Republicans to all of its seats, all winning by a huge margin if the race was contested at all. Voters choosing House candidates from the losing party in those two states wasted their vote; not a single one helped elect someone. For them, the monopoly politics of their state meant that voting was a waste of time. Twelve more states have such monopoly representation in the U.S. House, and ten other states are only one representative shy of monopoly representation, a total of twenty-four states.

The resulting monopoly politics not only affects representation—to the point where elected opposition has become a nearly extinct species in most states—but also creates a new classification: the "orphaned" voter. Orphaned voters are those Democrats and Republicans who, like the supporters of a third party anywhere and most nonwhite voters, are a geographic minority in an out-of-favor district or state with little hope of electing a representative. Orphaned voters have no electoral or governmental outlet for their political sympathies or passions.

It's not as if there aren't millions of Republican voters *living* in Democratic districts, and vice versa, all across the country. It's just that these orphaned voters—these geographic minorities—never win representation because, district after district, they don't have sufficient votes and are outvoted. For each individual contest, for each single-seat race, there are simply too many of one type of voter—Republicans in Nebraska or Idaho, say, or Democrats in Massachusetts or California or in most cities—overwhelming the other type of voter. For millions of orphaned voters across the United States, the act of voting does not result in their electing a representative. These voters have few prospects of electing someone in the near future. But they can have more impact by writing a check and mailing it to a candidate in a more competitive race somewhere else in the country.

Orphaned voters are smothered by the partisan avalanche that blankets the single-seat districts of their region or state. Consequently, the political cultures of these states and regions, which ideally should thrive on an exchange of ideas and public debate, have become a political monoculture, lacking the most basic level of political pluralism or public debate.[12]

One corrosive effect of the winner-take-all system and the gerrymandering of legislative districts is the understated impact on the psyche of voters and on their sense of whether their vote is important or politics is meaningful. During the redistricting process, most voters are plunked into a safe, one-party district, even a one-party state, and their vote becomes either superfluous (if their party dominates the district or state) or impotent (if they are an orphaned voter or geographic minority). Either way, the act of voting becomes a waste of time, and a cruel hoax to their democratic aspirations. Without opposition politics, which is being squelched by filtering natural partisan demographics through a twisted redistricting process and its incumbent protection racket, debate and discourse are disappearing, and with it the political ideas that are the seeds for tomorrow's solutions.

To be sure, for a handful of congressional races the 2001 redistricting process did shake things up a bit. A few incumbents whose districts changed substantially had to face many new voters; and for those states that lost seats during reapportionment a few incumbents from the same party were forced into the same districts and had to face each other for reelection, making for a few extremely bitter party primaries.[13] As researchers such as Harvard professor Gary King and University of California–Berkeley professor Andrew Gelman have stated, district elections likely would be even *less* competitive, particularly in the first subsequent election cycle or two, if redistricting never occurred at all. Yet with the line-drawing process and its effects so tumultuous and so much an insider's game, it's a strong indicator of how *defective* our winner-take-all electoral system is. The use of single-seat, winner-take-all districts with legislative lines redrawn by the incumbents and party leaders is a major factor contributing to the decline of our representative democracy. We can pass all the campaign finance reform we want, but it will scarcely change this fundamental reality of our political landscape. We condemn elections with one-party choice in places like Cuba and China; but with the redistricting of winner-take-all districts dividing the political map into winners and losers, any chance of a politics of inclusion, pluralism, debate, and discourse is immediately subverted.

The Gravity of the Prize: Winning More Than Your Fair Share

> Nothing Monica Lewinsky and Bill Clinton did together will ever have as much impact on election results as the partisan makeup of congressional districts around the country.
>
> —Rob Richie, *Center for Voting and Democracy*

> Redistricting will determine the future control of Congress.
>
> —Kevin Mack, *Democratic legislative campaign committee*

Redistricting is the window through which we may view something more profound and disturbing about our winner-take-all electoral system. Much as a comet brings to scientists periodic information from the far-flung reaches of the galaxy, the decennial line-drawings that occurred in 1991–92 and 2001–02 afforded us an opportunity for a rare insight into the workings of our clanking, antiquated, eighteenth-century electoral methods.

Specifically, the shenanigans unleashed by recent redistricting created numerous opportunities for party leaders to game the system in an attempt to win more than their fair share of seats. Only one side can win in a winner-take-all system, and both sides try rapaciously to manipulate the redistricting rules. The unsurprising results are "representation rip-offs" and "political power rip-offs," where one side gains unfairly as the bewildered public tries to follow along in what seems a House of Mirrors.

Here's how it works. In most states, whichever party completes the trifecta of winning control of the governor's seat as well as the state house and senate at the start of each decade wins the godlike power to redistrict their state's legislative district lines, not only for all their state's legislative seats but also for that state's U.S. House seats. By using techniques such as "packing" (whereby the lines are drawn so that you pack as many as possible of your political opponents' voters into a few districts and make the surrounding districts more favorable to your party) and "cracking" (where you split your opponent's supporters into two or more districts), those controlling the redistricting process can dramatically heighten the chance of winning more than their fair share of seats.

For instance, Republicans in Virginia completed the trifecta and dominated redistricting in early 2001; they were able to rig the district lines to win eight out of eleven U.S. House seats in a state that then elected a Democratic governor statewide.[14] In Florida, a state that is a toss-up statewide for president, governor, and U.S. senator, the GOP won the trifecta and parlayed it into districts that allowed them to win eighteen out of twenty-five House seats. In California, when Democrats regained control of the governor's seat in 1998 and completed the trifecta, they gained monopoly control over redrawing

California's 53 U.S. House seats—12 percent of the national total—and 120 state legislative seats, ensuring their landslide victory in more than 60 percent of the races.

Republican and Democratic analysts both say that control over the redistricting process gives a party such an advantage that the state legislative and gubernatorial elections in 1998 and 2000—not the Congressional elections or the presidential election—determined who will hold a majority in the U.S. House of Representatives right through 2010. Ironically, it is true that voters in 1998 and 2000 determined representation for voters throughout the next decade; they had more impact on who won state and congressional elections in the year 2002 and beyond than voters in 2002 did. In fact, numerous observers have stated that the outcome of the 1994 elections, when Republicans took control of Congress for the first time in forty years, was due in no small part to Republican gains made during the 1991–92 redistricting.[15]

So the battle to complete or prevent the trifecta is fierce, and this is why, while the public's attention was riveted on the face-off in 2000 between Al Gore and George W. Bush, the low-intensity conflict for control of the nation's statehouses was just as pivotal.[16] Despite the fundamental importance of these state legislative races at the end of each decade, for the most part they fly under the public's radar. But both parties were totally focused and engaged, committing unprecedented resources to end-of-the-decade legislative and gubernatorial races. They targeted a record-setting amount of money to those few races where it would make a difference, with spending on *state* legislative elections passing the billion-dollar mark for the first time in the 2000 elections.[17] The trench warfare was fought state by state, district by district, in a handful of close races—the Gettysburg of our political landscape.

The special election in Pennsylvania in June 2000 to fill a single vacant state house seat illustrates how important control of the state legislature is to the two major parties. With the Pennsylvania House tied at one hundred seats for each party (there were three vacancies), and with the GOP already in control of the state senate and the governor's mansion, Republicans were fighting to complete their trifecta and Democrats were fighting to prevent it. The lone seat in this special election was going to be the deciding race. The candidates spent millions of dollars, most of it raised from national campaign committees and outside sources. Vice President Gore campaigned in the district and President Bill Clinton recorded radio spots for the Democratic candidate. GOP Governor Tom Ridge and national Republicans actively supported the Republican candidate. Meanwhile, ninety-one of Pennsylvania's house candidates (45 percent) faced *no major party opponent* in November 2000, as the two parties ignored districts they could not possibly hope to win. (Coda: the GOP won that Pennsylvania seat, gaining control of redistricting and gerrymandered districts that resulted in Democrats losing three U.S. House seats.)[18]

A state legislature is often the best example of how natural partisan demographics filtered through contorted legislative districts can unfairly tilt a legislature toward one party or another. Using the presidential popular vote as an indicator of the number of Democratic and Republican voters in each state, we can compare the disproportion between the presidential vote and the number of legislative seats won by each party in a state legislature to arrive at a vote-to-seats ratio (the presidential popular vote is used rather than the aggregate statewide vote for each party in state legislative races because so many state legislative races are uncontested—37 percent in 2002 and 41 percent in 2000—which serves to depress the turnout total for a state legislative race).

Comparing the popular vote for Gore to the number of seats won by Democrats at the state legislative level, we find that the 29 percent of Idaho voters who pulled the Democratic tab for president in November 2000 ended up that year with only 13 percent of Democratic seats in the state House of Representatives. In essence, these voters won 16 percent less representation than their numbers would indicate they deserve. In Kansas, Democrats were similarly subsumed, winning 39 percent of the presidential vote but only 25 percent of state House seats. This disproportionality works both ways, naturally, and in Rhode Island Republican voters accumulated about 34 percent of the presidential vote for Bush, but ended up with only 16 percent of the state representation, a representation rip-off of 18 percent. In Maryland, 42 percent of voters pulled Bush, approaching a majority, but they ended up with only 25 percent of the Republican state House seats, a rip-off of 17 percent. In Massachusetts, 35 percent of voters pulling Republican in the presidential race won only 14 percent of state House seats, a huge representation rip-off of 21 percent.[19]

The bitter partisan divide is exacerbated by this representation rip-off, as one side effectively wins more representation and political power than it deserves, while the other side is frustrated and unfairly marginalized. Oftentimes the representation rip-off produces an undeserved veto-proof majority that can ram through radical policies without a popular mandate. In Utah, where Republicans in 2000 won 69 percent of state house and senate seats, Democrats were so shut out by the representation rip-off that they threatened to quit running candidates to amplify the unfairness of one-party politics. "The reality is we live in a one-party state," said Democratic Party leader Scott Howell. "Maybe it's time to have no Democrats in the Legislature . . . make Utahans wake up to what local political life would be like with no alternative voice, no alternative power, to the majority Republicans."[20] The fact is, in states encumbered by monopoly politics such as Utah, Idaho, and Massachusetts, the partisan redistricting of winner-take-all, single-seat districts is producing a victorious majority who lord over the vanquished minority in what can only be described as a kind of political feudalism. These winner-take-all districts are exacerbating an emerging trend of bitter partisan division and regional balkanization, the infamous Red and Blue America, where one political party dominates an entire state or region and political opposition is effectively snuffed out.

The Soft Money Kings and Queens

> Redistricting makes the inequities in campaign financing even worse. Most elections are so noncompetitive due to how the lines are drawn that big donors already know who's going to win. So they give to the likely winners to curry favor.
>
> —Professor Douglas Amy, *political scientist*[21]

The catastrophic impact of redistricting goes beyond reducing competition, protecting the incumbent, undermining voter engagement, and deciding which party wins a majority. It also gives a distorted shape to the flow of political influence, money, and power and greases the wheels of the political machine.

The partition of the winner-take-all map into competitive versus noncompetitive races creates a fund-raising pecking order in which safe-seat incumbents are rewarded for raising excess campaign funds that can be handed off to a colleague in a closer race. These Soft Money Kings and Queens sit atop the soft money pile, dispensing favors and collecting fealty, both within their own personal safe districts and within the legislature, and then sprinkle their booty around to targeted races, buying themselves higher ranking in the party pecking order. This is how a political machine or fiefdom is created and maintained, with all its progenies of patronage, logrolling, and pork doling.

The geographic-based nature of our winner-take-all system combined with the redistricting roulette *define* this pyramidal shape to our political landscape and permit this kind of gaming and manipulation to occur. The fundamentally noncompetitive nature of most district races acts as a kind of lens that collects money from all over the country and focuses it on a few races where it can have overwhelming impact. Especially at a time when control of the U.S. House is likely to hang in the balance each election for the foreseeable future, it means that a handful of political leaders (DeLay, Hastert, Frost, Pelosi, Kennedy, and the like) will each be able to maintain his or her own well-oiled political machine.[22] The party leaders' role starts resembling that of a Mafioso *don*, dispensing favors and cash and making decisions with victory-or-defeat ramifications for their party; to the victor belongs the spoils *and* the turf. This dynamic is much more distorting of our democracy than simply money buying elections, because it concentrates power in a small number of hands and Rolodexes.

The importance of these party leadership PACs helps explain the seeming paradox of thousands of noncompetitive safe seats amid a sea of soft money and campaign millions. Voters see headline after headline screaming about all the hundreds of millions of dollars that are spent on elections, about the Democrats and Republicans holding gold-plated fundraisers, raising money from the same corporate clients in the incessant drive to win majority control of the legislatures. Things certainly *sound* competitive, and politics certainly *appears* bought and sold by big money donors. Yet most voters' experience is that of living in a safe, one-party district. Most races are decidedly noncompetitive, often even uncontested, because of the lopsided partisan composition of the district. Says Burdett Loomis, a political scientist at the University of Kansas: "A lot of money will flow to a relative handful of seats. In those seats, it's nuclear war. Twenty miles away, there's nothing."[23]

The real battle is focused on those seats on which control of the legislature, and all the perks and power that come with it, depends. For that effort, party leaders raise gobs of soft money and sprinkle it around, calling the shots. Donors place their bets on candidates they *know* will win, because the winner-take-all districts have been drawn to produce that result. Rather than trying to buy elections per se, donors try to buy access to legislative leaders, and in some cases a chance to actually author important legislation. The passage of the McCain-Feingold legislation, which bans soft money, offers some hope, but after passage opponents quickly began conspiring to undermine it, both in the courts and by finding other legal means to circumvent its prescriptions. Trying to stop the flow of money is like trying to stop a river with a net.

All of these dynamics are unleashed by the geographic-based, winner-take-all, single-seat district system. Whichever party, Democrat or Republican, dominates a particular district is often decided years beforehand, in the backroom game of cards in which incumbent politicians and party bosses supervise redrawing of district lines. The preponderance of safe seats leaves the handful of close races as the small postage stamp of political real estate where political war is waged, and where campaign ordnance is bombarded. In a nation so closely divided, whichever side wins more of these skirmishes for the swing districts wins the big prize: majority control of the various legislatures; control over committees, subcommittees, and budget and tax policy; and control over redistricting in those states.

The 2001–02 redistricting was perhaps the most flagrantly abusive we have ever seen. In part, the GOP has emerged as the national winner at the state and federal levels because since 1991 they have been smarter and more strategic in the redistricting process, used emerging redistricting computer technologies better, and better targeted their resources to the right state and federal races. No other single factor, not even campaign finance inequity, has played so large a role in defining our winner-take-all system as this redistricting of geographic-based, single-seat districts. The resulting electoral barrenness—produced by the ennui of predictability, the stark lack of competition, the orphaning of millions of voters, the loss of political debate and ideas, and the distortion of legislative majorities—is where voter capitulation and an alarming postdemocracy begin. If this isn't a bizarre way to run a democracy, then what is?

Notes

1. Senator McDaniel is quoted in Hoeffel, J. "Six Incumbents Are a Week Away from Easy Election." *Winston-Salem Journal*, Jan. 27, 1998.

2. The origin of the term *gerrymander* has been oft-told, but it bears repeating. It was coined after the name of a Massachusetts governor, Eldridge Gerry, who in 1812 approved the efforts

of the Jeffersonian-dominated legislature to create a famously contorted district that split Essex County in an effort to dilute the strength of the Federalists. Noting the resemblance of the new, oddly shaped district to a salamander, a local newspaper dubbed the creation a "gerrymander." Thus was produced the term of art that has passed down through the centuries.

3. Pamela Karlan, professor of law at Stanford University, videotaped testimony at public hearings on "Race, Reapportionment and Redistricting" in San Francisco in September 1997; the videos were followed by videotaped interview.

4. See, for instance, Monmonier, M. *Bushmanders and Bullwinkles: How Politicians Manipulate Electronic Maps and Census Data to Win Elections.* Chicago: University of Chicago Press, 2001.

5. See anecdotes related in Gelman, A., and King, G. "Enhancing Democracy through Legislative Redistricting." *American Political Science Review,* 1994, 88(3), p. 541.

6. Quach, H. K., and Bunis, D. "All Bow to Redistrict Architect: Politics Secretive, Single-Minded Michael Berman Holds All the Crucial Cards." *Orange County Register,* Aug. 26, 2001, p. 1.

7. The results were similar for the 2000 and 1998 House elections. In 1998, 90 percent of races were won by a comfortable victory margin greater than ten points and 73 percent were won by a landslide margin greater than twenty points, as 98 percent of incumbents won reelection, and the average margin of victory for the incumbent was a whopping 43 percent. See "Monopoly Politics 2002: How 'No Choice' Elections Rule in a Competitive House," published on the Web by the Center for Voting and Democracy (www.fairvote.org/2002/ index.html).

8. 2002 and 2000 were not atypical. In 1998, there was no Democrat or no Republican candidate in 41.1 percent of the state legislative races; in 1996, 32.7 percent; in 1994, 35.8 percent; and in 1992, 32.8 percent. See "Dems, Reps Failed to Nominate in 2000." *Ballot Access News,* 2000, 16(9), p. 2 (published by Richard Winger, P.O. Box 470296, San Francisco, CA 94147, ban@igc.org).

9. See "Monopoly Politics 2002."

10. See "Voter Participation and Victory Margins, 1994 Elections, U.S. House of Representatives, and Dubious Democracy 2001" (www.fairvote.org/reports/1999/overview.htm), reports published by the Center for Voting and Democracy.

11. See Heilprin, J. "105.4 Million Voters Cast Ballots." Associated Press, Dec. 18, 2000. Also see the report released by Curtis Gans and the Committee for the Study of the American Electorate, in "Voter Turnout Rose in 2000, But No Lasting Impact Is Seen," *New York Times,* p. A12.

12. Some political commentators protest against viewing Republican and Democratic voters in terms of a partisan monolith, pointing out that not all Republican voters are always head-over-heels sold on the Republican candidate, or Democratic voters on the Democratic candidate, which is certainly true. But if their only other viable choice is the other major party, many consider it going too far in the opposite direction, and so they keep within the fold, voting the lesser of two evils, albeit begrudgingly. Their politics is defined by voting against a particular candidate or party more than by being for anything. More and more Americans vote with this kind of negative consent in mind. Because of this dynamic, the pattern followed by most voters is increasingly consistent and predictable over time—as political observers have come to realize.

13. For example, after Indiana lost a Congressional seat in the 2000 census, a Democratic-dominated commission redrew the Congressional district boundaries so that two Republicans were forced to vie for the same seat in the 2002 primaries. Both were staunchly conservative Republicans and erstwhile allies, but once lumped in the same district a real catfight broke out, driven by the rawest of political impulses: survival. The intraparty feuding became so intense that Rep. Thomas Davis of Virginia, the chairman of the National Republican Congressional Committee, commented: "They don't help matters by going and carving each other up on a personal basis every day. [They] are gaming this in an inappropriate fashion." Well beyond Indiana, individual battles brewed in other states. "It's a very selfish enterprise," Davis said; "it's every man for himself." Berke, R. L. "Democrats' New Map of Indiana Divides GOP." *New York Times,* June 2, 2001.

14. White, R. "Strategy Aims to Keep Foe's Voters at Home." *Fairfax* (Va.) *Journal,* Nov. 2, 1999, p. A1. See also "No Contest, No Choice" (editorial), *USA Today,* Nov. 3, 1999, p. 30A.

15. Curran, T., and Mercurio, J. "Parties Brace for Looming Remaps: Governors, State Legislators Hold Keys to Members' Fates." *Roll Call*, Mar. 19, 1998. For instance, Mark Gersh, Washington director of the National Committee for an Effective Congress and a consultant to the Democratic Congressional Campaign Committee, is quoted as saying, "I would attribute about 60 percent of the gains Republicans made [in the House since 1990] to redistricting." Morton Kondracke, a columnist for *Roll Call*, estimated that fewer than twelve thousand voters nationwide—0.06 percent of the eligible voting population—swung the 1994 vote to the House Republicans.

16. Control of a state legislature also dramatically affects the competitiveness of an election. A 1995 report entitled "The Mapmakers and Competitiveness" by the Center for Voting and Democracy assessed the impact of the 1991–92 redistricting by comparing the 1992 and 1994 congressional elections with the 1990 elections. The study found that in the seventeen states where one party had a trifecta there was an average 7.5 percent increase in the number of competitive elections (elections won with less than 55 percent of the vote) from 1990 to 1994. But in states with split party control of the legislature, there was a 22 percent increase (nearly a threefold rise) in the number of competitive elections in the same years.

17. Greenblatt, A. "The Mapmaking Mess." *Governing*, Jan. 2001, p. 21. See also the report by Brigham Young University's Center for the Study of Elections and Democracy that looked at soft money expenditures and issue advocacy in the 2000 election. The report concluded that the battle for control of the U.S. Congress was concentrated on relatively few races, in which candidates raised and spent a record-setting amount of money. The political parties—(through soft money) and interest groups—(through election issue advocacy, independent expenditures, and internal communications) effectively doubled the money spent on campaign communications in these contests. The report also noted that closing the party soft money exemption from contribution limits merely produces a tremendous incentive for individuals and groups to shift to issue advocacy and independent expenditures. Report quoted in the *Political Standard*, newsletter of the Alliance for Better Campaigns, 2001, 4(1), p. 2.

18. Information on Pennsylvania is from the Website of the National Conference of State Legislatures (www.ncsl.org/ncsldb/elect98/profile.cfm?yearsel=2000&statesel=PA).

19. If anything, these figures probably understate the case, since Gore was disproportionately unpopular out west; his vote in Montana, say, was far less than that for relatively progressive Democratic candidates for the House and Senate. In Massachusetts, Republicans actually won the last three statewide races for governor, yet they have only 14 percent of seats in the Massachusetts state house.

20. Janofsky, M. "Utah GOP Endangers a Democrat." *New York Times*, Nov. 23, 2001. See also Bernick, B., Jr. "Will Utah Demos Run No Legislative Candidates at All in 2000?" *Desert News*, Mar., 27, 1998.

21. Videotaped interview at Race, Reapportionment, and Redistricting conference, Minneapolis, Nov. 1997.

22. VandeHei, J., and Curran, T. "Parties Pushing for Early Money: DeLay Plans to Distribute $1M to 10 Members." *Roll Call*, June 16, 1999. See also Freedberg, L. "Pelosi Raises $3 Million for Democrats." *San Francisco Chronicle*, Oct. 14, 2000, p. A1; Hook, J. "A Kennedy Pursues Money Side of the Family Business." *Los Angeles Times*, July 3, 2000.

23. Quoted in Hook, J. "Handful of Seats Could Sway Battle over House." *Los Angeles Times*, Jan. 17, 2000, p. A1.

Steven Hill is senior analyst for the Center for Voting and Democracy and author of Fixing Elections: The Failure of America's Winner-Take-All Politics.

Redistricting Reforms

Eric C. Olson

As long as our political system uses winner-take-all, single-seat districts, there will be an obvious need to reform the redistricting process. But the public interest, rather than narrow political interests, should drive redistricting. Which approaches hold the most promise?

Public Watchdog

Make the redistricting process a very public one, with full news media coverage and citizen input. Don't let redistricting happen behind closed doors, where incumbents can pay $20,000 in protection money to the people who draw the lines, to draw them a safe seat.

Public Interest Redistricting

At a minimum, the redistricting process must be taken out of the hands of the politicians and party leaders. Several states have adopted criteria-driven, independent redistricting commissions, which engage in a more public-interest-oriented redistricting that offers examples of how to return the process to the public. Here are a few recent examples of public interest redistricting.

Washington. In the 1991–92 redistricting, Washington State used a nonpartisan, criteria-driven commission to draw congressional and state legislative districts, resulting in some of the nation's most competitive U.S. House elections of the 1990s. Washington State had seven races during the 1990s that were decided by a margin of less than 5 percent; another eight contests resulted in a margin of victory between 5 and 10 percent. Congressional incumbents lost in five of the state's nine districts during the decade, and the balance between the parties changed in every election.

Iowa. Iowa uses a three-step process to draw congressional and state legislative districts, involving civil servants, an independent commission, and the state legislature. The first step is directed by civil servants at the state Legislative Services Bureau, which is charged with coming up with three sets of district maps for each legislative body. This bureaucratic task cannot use partisan information, and it may consider only (1) population equality, (2) contiguity, (3) unity of counties and cities, and (4) geographic compactness of the district, in that order of importance. The second step is that these three map sets for each legislative body are given to a five-member commission, called the Temporary Redistricting Advisory Commission. The commission must recommend to the legislature which of the three sets should be adopted. The Democratic and Republican parties each choose two members of the commission (who cannot be partisan officeholders), and those four members choose the fifth member. At least three public hearings must be conducted by the commission around the state.

A plan for each legislative body is recommended to the state legislature, which can only vote them up or down without amendments. If the legislature rejects a set, it must give its reasons, and the Legislative Services Bureau then sends another set to the Temporary Redistricting Advisory Commission and repeats the process. If all three sets are opposed by the legislature, the latter may create its own plan; this possibility is remote, however, because it would be seen as a partisan attempt to hijack the process and provoke a voter backlash. Once a plan is accepted by the legislature, the governor retains the ability to veto, but this would restart the process and again might provoke a voter backlash. With Iowa's commission method, the state has enjoyed meaningful elections and partisan competition; incumbents have not been immune to close contests. In 2002, for example, three of Iowa's five House races were competitive, and only one race was won by a landslide.

New Jersey. New Jersey also employs a commission method of drawing up districts, called the New Jersey Apportionment Commission (NJAC). However, the commission is bipartisan rather than nonpartisan, composed of an equal number of Democrats and Republicans, and it exhibits flaws as a result. Also, the commission is not prevented from using partisan data, though it must use other criteria such as preserving contiguity and compactness as well. The chairperson of each political party appoints five members. The ten-member NJAC must reach an agreement on a redistricting plan within a specified period. Both parties try to preserve their party's districts, which creates some statewide balance of representation between Republicans and Democrats.

If the NJAC fails to reach an agreement by the deadline, a neutral eleventh member from the public is appointed by the chief justice of the state Supreme Court and is charged with moving the two parties to an agreement by a new deadline. In the case of an even split, the public member casts a deciding vote; the governor may veto the congressional plan (but not the state legislative plan). Critics of the New Jersey method, which was adopted in 1966, note that introducing partisan data in drawing districts has done relatively little to prevent creation of numerous noncompetitive seats and safe-seat incumbents. New Jersey's redistricting method is "fair" only to the Democratic and Republican parties and their incumbents, who may be happy to get their share of the seats in the state, but it is not fair to voters who desire a real choice.

Arizona. The citizens of Arizona passed Proposition 106, which handed the task of redistricting the congressional and state legislative districts to the Arizona Independent Redistricting Commission. This is a five-member body, with one commissioner each appointed by the state speaker of the House, the House minority leader, the president of the Senate, and the Senate minority leader. The fifth member is not affiliated with a political party and is selected by the other four members. The Independent Redistricting Commission is charged with redrawing fair, competitive districts on the basis of criteria set forth in Proposition 106: compactness, contiguity, and respect for existing boundaries such as cities, geographic features, and "communities of interest." Meetings of the redistricting commission are open to the public, and there are several ways citizens can influence the commission—by e-mail, at meetings, or online. The redistricting commission makes drafts of the preliminary maps available online.

Single-Seat Districts

Are single-seat districts redeemable? Public interest redistricting is better than leaving the process in the hands of incumbents and party leaders, but using winner-take-all, single-seat districts still creates problems. Even the best public-interest redistricting in the hands of an independent commission guided by fair, nonpolitical criteria—although it would certainly introduce more competition into some congressional races—still leaves most voters living in districts with noncompetitive contests and safe-seat incumbents.

Full Representation

Ultimately, the solution is to convert the U.S.-style winner-take-all voting system to a full-representation (also called proportional representation) system. This means breaking up the single-seat districts and creating multiseat districts, where, for example, if a political party wins 20 percent of the popular vote its candidates win 20 percent of the legislative seats. Full-representation systems are used by most of the world's established democracies; the lack of winner-take-all-single-seat districts make it much harder to gerrymander districts or deprive voters of the ability to make effective choices. Using full representation produces more competitive elections and allows more voters to have a fair chance to win representation.

Illinois' state legislature used such a system for 110 years (it was changed in 1980), and the *Chicago Tribune* has written that "it produced some of the best and brightest in Illinois politics." A bipartisan commission, chaired by former Democratic congressman Abner Mikvah and former Republican governor Jim Edgar, concluded that junking the single-seat district system and returning to Illinois' full system would increase competition and voter choice, decrease bitter partisanship, and decrease regional balkanization between cities and the rest of the state. Those are benefits that our national politics could use as well.

Eric C. Olson is a former legislative aide for Congressman Bernie Sanders and former deputy director of the Center for Voting and Democracy.

New Means for Political Empowerment in the Asian Pacific American Community

Steven Hill, Robert Richie

In recent years, alternatives to winner-take-all systems have advanced from being controversial to becoming a credible option for the political empowerment of racial minority communities. On their own merits, and as a strategic response to U.S. Supreme Court rulings on voting rights and redistricting as well as to shifting demographic trends, full-representation voting methods (sometimes called proportional voting) such as choice voting, cumulative voting, and limited voting are increasingly used and recognized as means to increase minority representation in local, state, and even federal elections.[1] Not only can full representation be an effective vehicle for increasing fair minority representation but it can also create incentives for other good government values, including more voter participation, a broader range of strong candidacies, and an appropriate balance between jurisdictionwide interests and narrower neighborhood interests.

To better understand the value of full representation for all racial minorities, this article focuses on the case for the Asian Pacific American (APA) community, which often finds itself dispersed over a geographic area and thus not concentrated enough to elect an APA candidate from the drawing of single-member districts. In fact, in Los Angeles, New York City, and San Francisco, three major cities with large populations of APAs, the traditional voting-rights strategy of drawing a majority-minority district has generally failed APAs, because they currently hold only two (one of which may be lost in a December 2002 runoff in San Francisco) out of a total of seventy-seven city council seats elected by single-seat districts in these three cities. Evidence from New York City, Los Angeles, and San Francisco shows that representation for APAs would have a much higher chance of success using full-representation voting systems. We examine the electoral prospects for APAs using these alternative systems and propose strategies to seek their adoption.

Political Representation for Racial Minorities

Experts suggest that 95 percent of black representation and the majority of Latino, APA, and Native American representation in the coming decade was already effectively won or lost in the 2001–02 round of redistricting. Dependence on redistricting to provide representation to communities of color is based on three factors: white voters' general preference for white candidates, the fact that people of color are in the minority in most areas, and the general use in the United States of winner-take-all methods of voting in which a 50.1 percent majority in a given constituency wins all representation in its area. Without a substantial number of racial minority voters in winner-take-all districts, few racial minority candidates will win. The absence of a single black or Latino member in the U.S. Senate is one clear example of the impact of race on representation: although African Americans and Latinos make up a quarter of our population, no state has a black or Latino majority.

The 2002 congressional elections brought no increase in African American representation, a decrease in APA representation, and only a small growth in Latino representation. This status quo election was in stark contrast to 1992, when the last redistricting sparked a growth of more than 50 percent in African American, Latino, and APA representation, which points to the limitations of a winner-take-all voting system in promoting fair representation of our nation's diversity. Table 1 demonstrates that at the congressional level growth of minority representation has stalled. Trends are similar in state and local elections.

We believe it is high time to explore vigorously the alternative of full representation. In the decade since Lani Guinier's nomination to head the civil rights division of the Department of Justice, full representation voting systems have become a credible alternative for political empowerment. The voting section of the civil rights division has approved adoption of full-representation voting systems in more than seventy-five jurisdictions, including use of cumulative voting for school board elections in Amarillo, Texas, a city of more than 160,000 people. In Texas, more than fifty jurisdictions now use cumulative voting, with the number steadily growing in the wake of then-governor George W. Bush's signing of legislation in 1995 to allow school districts to adopt cumulative voting and limited voting.[2] In 1999, the Department of Justice (DOJ) wrote an amicus brief backing a federal judge's order of cumulative voting for elections to the city council and park board in Chicago Heights, Illinois. In September 1999, a representative of the DOJ's civil rights division testified

Table 1. Race of U.S. House Members

Year	Black	Latino	APA
1982	19	8	3
1992	38	17	4
2002	37	23	3

in favor of a bill in Congress that would allow states to use full-representation systems to elect their congressional representatives. After hearing persuasive evidence from the Asian American Legal Defense and Education Fund (AALDEF), the DOJ denied preclearance to New York City after the state legislature sought to replace choice voting, a fully proportional voting system, with a less proportional system for electing the city's local school boards.[3] In its denial, the DOJ noted that the school boards had a significantly higher percentage of all racial minorities than any other legislative body in the city and were the only level of election where APAs have had electoral success in New York.

The logic of full-representation voting systems for minority representation is too compelling to be held down for long, particularly in the wake of court rulings striking down majority-minority districts,[4] the so-called *Shaw* rulings.[5] Indeed, full-representation systems may have special utility for the APA community, which often finds itself dispersed over a geographic area and therefore not concentrated enough to benefit from majority-minority districts.[6] In fact, in Los Angeles, New York City, and San Francisco the traditional voting rights strategy of drawing majority-minority districts has failed. Evidence suggests that the electoral prospects for APAs would improve significantly using a strategy other than the single-seat district—namely, a multiseat district elected by a full-representation voting system.[7]

APA Electoral Success in New York City School Board Elections

The principle behind a full-representation, proportional system is simple: any grouping of like-minded voters should win legislative seats in proportion to its share of the popular vote (see the Appendix for more details about various full-representation systems). Whereas our current winner-take-all principle awards 100 percent of the representation to a 50.1 percent majority, a full-representation system allows voters in a minority to win a proportional share of representation.[8] For example, five one-seat districts could be combined into a single five-seat district. If APA voters constitute 20 percent of the vote in this five-seat district, they could elect at least one of the five seats—even if voting were polarized entirely along racial lines—rather than be shut out, as they would be in a traditional at-large election or in a district-based system where APAs are geographically dispersed.[9]

New York City is a good example for comparing the impact that full-representation voting systems and geographic-based district elections can have on APA electoral success. When it came time in 1991 to draw the electoral district map for New York's newly expanded city council, it was possible to create council districts that represented the interests of African Americans, Caribbean-born blacks, Puerto Ricans, Dominicans, and all sorts of white subgroups (ranging from ethnic whites to Hasidim, the gay community of

Greenwich Village, conservative Republicans on Staten Island, and limousine liberals on the Upper West Side). With APAs making up 7 percent of New York's population, three seats drawn for APAs on New York City's fifty-one-seat city council might have seemed plausible, or at least one seat corresponding with the 2.3 percent APA share of registered voters in 1993. But there was no single geographic concentration of APA voters in New York City large enough to form a majority APA district. Many APAs live in APA communities—in Chinatown or in parts of Queens—but those neighborhoods were not linked to one another in a way that could create a compact electoral district.[10]

The only elections in New York City where APAs achieved electoral success before the 2001 city council elections were those for the thirty-two local school boards. Those positions have been elected by a multiseat full-representation voting system called choice voting.[11] After the DOJ denied a change to a plan that would have more than tripled the percentage of voter support necessary to win a seat, choice voting was retained for the May 1999 elections. Of twenty-one APA candidates who ran, fifteen were successful, winning seats in nine of the thirty-two boards and winning 5 percent of school board seats overall.[12]

The rapidly increasing participation and success of APA candidates in school board elections is an excellent example of how full representation, and choice voting in particular, serves to bring new voices and fresh faces into New York's elections and legislative bodies. APAs have had nearly continuous representation on the boards since 1975, even though no APAs have won any other electoral office in the state or city. But after 1986, participation and electoral success took a dramatic upward swing. The number of APA winners doubled to four in 1989, then rose to seven in 1993 (out of eleven APA candidates), to eleven winners (out of fifteen) in 1996, and to fifteen (out of twenty-one) in 1999.[13]

Choice voting made these successes possible even though APAs make up less than 20 percent of the adult population in every school district. This is because with nine seats on each school board, using a full-representation system such as choice voting means that only about 10 percent of the vote is required to win one seat, 20 percent to win two, and so on.[14] Also, choice voting uses what is known as a "transferable ballot" (ranking candidates 1, 2, 3, and so on). If a voter's first choice doesn't win, the vote is counted for (transferred to) the second choice. These transferable ballots are extremely valuable because they promote coalition building, prevent voters from splitting their vote among similar candidates (competing APA candidates) or supposedly wasting their vote on a losing candidate, and allow voters to choose the candidates they really like instead of the lesser of two evils. These qualities promote participation and engagement, spurring APAs to run even where they constitute less than 10 percent of the population, and to run enough candidates to win three of nine seats in two districts. Choice voting has amounted to a similar gateway for other newly organized communities in the city, including, in recent years, immigrant communities from Russia and the Dominican Republic.

Use of choice voting for New York's city council elections, instead of the current system of fifty-one single-member districts, almost certainly would lead to several APA victories and an increased number of APA candidates. Voter registration data suggest that APAs would have won at least two seats in the 2001 city council elections if choice voting were used in each of the city's five boroughs, and more seats as the decade progressed. Even where APA candidates were not successful, their decision to run (which would likely happen in every borough in the city if choice voting were adopted) would help the APA community define and articulate its interests, raise visibility, and find allies in the non-APA community.

Full Representation in Practice

Here are a few examples of other localities where full-representation voting systems are making a difference.

Amarillo, Texas. In the spring of 1999, the Amarillo (Texas) Independent School District, representing a population of more than 160,000 people, adopted cumulative voting. Although cumulative voting does not have all the desirable qualities of choice voting (such as ranked ballots), it does lower the threshold of support necessary to win as much as choice voting. African Americans and Latinos in Amarillo together make up a quarter of the city's population, but no African American or Latino candidate had won a seat on the school board in decades. Instituted to settle a voting rights lawsuit involving the Mexican American Legal Defense and Educational Fund, the League of United Latin American Citizens, and the National Association for the Advancement of Colored People, cumulative voting had an immediate impact in the first cumulative voting election in May 2000. An African American candidate and a Latino candidate won seats with strong support in their respective communities, voter turnout increased more than three times over the most recent school board election, and all parties in the voting rights settlement expressed satisfaction with the new system.

In May 2002, another Latina was elected, which means the board now has four white representatives, two Latina, and one African American, in stark contrast to the all-white boards elected for the previous two decades. More than fifty Texas jurisdictions adopted cumulative voting in the 1990s alone. In 1995, Texas governor George W. Bush signed legislation that allows school districts to adopt cumulative voting and limited voting.

Alabama, New Mexico, and South Dakota. Cumulative voting and limited voting have also been used in nearly two dozen localities in Alabama for a decade, as well as localities in Alamogordo, New Mexico, and Sisseton, South Dakota.[15] Studies by various political scientists of the elections in Alabama demonstrate that they have boosted turnout and increased African

American representation as much as (or more than) would have occurred if single-seat districts had been used instead.[16] Another study by political scientist Jerome Gray found that more women were elected as well.[17]

African American candidate Bobby Agee, in 1988, was the highest vote-getter in the first elections using cumulative voting for a seven-seat commission in Chilton County, Alabama, even though African Americans made up barely 10 percent of the population and even though he was outspent more than twenty to one by the highest-spending candidate. Most of his supporters, overwhelmingly African American, took advantage of their opportunity to cast (or "cumulate") all seven of their votes for him rather than spread their votes among other candidates. The first African American commissioner in Chilton County's history, Agee has been reelected three times and has several times been selected by his white colleagues to be chair of the commission.[18]

Peoria, Illinois. Peoria, Illinois, the quintessential city of "middle America," uses cumulative voting for its city council elections. African Americans make up only 20 percent of the city's population, but African American candidates have won seats in all three elections in which cumulative voting has been used since a voting rights settlement in 1988.

Case Study One: Los Angeles City Council Elections

The city of Los Angeles is a textbook example of a situation where geographic dispersal of the APA vote prevents APAs from achieving the type of electoral success they have enjoyed in the New York City community school board elections, or elsewhere, as just described. Los Angeles also illustrates nicely how a full-representation system in a multiseat district allows the APA vote to become electorally competitive.

Los Angeles has fifteen city council districts, each electing one councilor representing more than 232,000 people—nearly half the size of a congressional district. APAs are about 10 percent of the voting age population of Los Angeles, and no more than 19 percent of the voting age population (1990 census data) in any one city council district. In most districts, APAs amount to far less than 19 percent. Not surprisingly, Los Angeles City Council has no elected APAs, despite a significant increase in the APA population since the 1990 census. Latinos constitute 35 percent of the voting age population according to 1990 census data, and they hold three seats on the city council. African Americans are 13 percent of the city's voting age population (1990 census data) but are highly concentrated geographically and also have three (20 percent of) city council seats. Whites are, not surprisingly, overrepresented, holding nine seats (60 percent) with only 42 percent of the voting age population.[19]

The current plan of fifteen single-seat districts for the Los Angeles city council clearly is a barrier to political representation for APAs, but as a number of examples illustrate, the electoral possibilities for APA voters are far less bleak when using multiseat districts and a full-representation voting system.

In fact, in two scenarios, APAs actually reach a threshold of electoral viability and competitiveness.

Three-Seat Districts in Los Angeles. If three single-seat city council districts were combined into one three-seat district using a full-representation system such as choice voting, any cohesive voting constituency greater than 25 percent could elect a candidate.[20] Smaller constituencies can elect a candidate by forming a coalition with other similar constituencies. Accordingly, if we combine some conglomeration of three contiguous city council districts having the highest APA populations, we find that the APA vote creeps closer to the victory threshold of 25 percent. For instance, combining city council districts 1, 13, and 14, we arrive at this ethnic composition: APAs, 15 percent; Latinos, 64 percent; African Americans, 3 percent; and whites, 17 percent.

Note that, compared to single-seat districts, in this three-seat district the APA vote is on a relative par with the white vote in terms of reaching the victory threshold of 25 percent. With lower voter turnout in the APA community, it would still be a challenge for APAs to elect a seat, but it is more possible than under a single-member district plan. APAs would form a powerful influence vote for a successful candidate to court.

Using other combinations of three-seat districts (for instance, combining districts 1, 4, and 13; or districts 4, 10, and 13; or districts 10, 13, and 14) would lead to similar results. Latinos and whites generally have the best shot at winning the three seats, with the third seat sometimes being very competitive for APAs, as well as for Latinos and African Americans. Whichever constituency could mobilize its voters and build a successful electoral coalition would win the seat. In other words, although the number of APAs would still fall short of the victory threshold of 25 percent, they would have a fighting chance to win in this three-seat district and would certainly be influential, particularly compared to the current scheme of fifteen single-seat districts.

Five-Seat Districts in Los Angeles. Even more interesting possibilities arise for APA voters in Los Angeles if the fifteen city council districts are combined into three five-seat districts. Under such a scheme, the APA community's chances of winning a seat on the Los Angeles City Council improve dramatically. A five-seat district would have a victory threshold of just under 17 percent of the vote.[21] Combining city council districts 1, 4, 10, 13, and 14, the overall ethnic composition becomes as follows: APAs, 15 percent; Latinos, 51 percent; African Americans, 10 percent; and whites, 23 percent.

In this scenario, the APA vote has almost reached the victory threshold. Needing some 17 percent of the vote to win a seat means that Latino voters should win two or three seats, and the white voters should win one or two. This leaves one seat still to be filled, and the APA vote is in its best position yet to do so. This would be a very competitive district for APAs, facilitating mobilization of APA candidates, voters, and resources.

These simulations are calculated using voting age population based on 1990 census data. Most experts agree that the APA population has increased significantly relative to other populations in Los Angeles, especially compared to whites and African Americans. Thus it is likely that the immediate chances of APA electoral success in a multiseat full-representation system are even better than estimated here. Also, these simulations assume that APAs vote in blocs or tend to support one particular candidate. Such a generalization is never entirely accurate, and it is perhaps less true for APAs than for Latinos and African Americans, but racially polarized voting is certainly an on-the-ground reality that has contributed to APAs being able to compete electorally in New York City school board elections. Still, intraethnic competition must be factored into any estimates of electoral viability.

Case Study Two: San Francisco Elections for County Board of Supervisors

For the 2000 county elections, San Francisco switched to a system of eleven single-seat districts from an at-large plurality system electing eleven seats to the Board of Supervisors. During these elections, APAs suffered a dramatic decline in representation, from three seats to one.[22] APAs constitute approximately 30 percent (1990 census data) of the city's population, but in 2000 they won only 9 percent of the representation owing to geographic dispersion of the APA population and the fact that the Chinatown district, drawn as a majority-minority Asian district (55 percent APA, 1990 census), actually elected a white liberal, not an Asian. The lone APA supervisor, an incumbent, instead was elected from the Asian-leaning Sunset district (46 percent APA).

If we combine three single-seat districts in San Francisco into one three-seat district (as we did in the Los Angeles case study) with a 25 percent victory threshold, we see a much different story. For instance, combining supervisorial districts 1, 4, and 7 we discover that APAs are about 40 percent of that three-seat district area and whites about 49 percent. If we combine supervisorial districts 3, 6, and 10, we find that APAs constitute about 37 percent of this multiseat district, with whites at 28 percent, African Americans at 18 percent, and Latinos at 11 percent. In both of these three-seat districts, APAs would elect at least one seat per district and possibly two, for a total of two to four seats. Combining districts 8, 9, and 11 produces a three-seat district with an APA population of 21 percent, another competitive district for APAs possibly to win one seat or certainly to be influential. Thus, full representation likely would significantly boost APA electoral success in San Francisco, just as it would in Los Angeles and New York City.

Addressing Concerns about Full-Representation Systems

In this section, we address a few common questions and concerns raised about full-representation voting systems.

- *Will larger districts make it more expensive and therefore more difficult for minority candidates to run?* No. Under a full-representation system, minorities have been able to win their fair share of representation in numerous elections, even when outspent. They are able to do this because, with a full-representation system, a successful candidate needs a smaller percentage of votes to win. Agee finished first in his Chilton County election, even though he was greatly outspent, by asking supporters to cumulate all their votes for him. Studies by our Center for Voting and Democracy and Democracy South found that in North Carolina and Vermont, both of which use a mix of one-seat districts and multi-seat districts, candidates actually have spent *less money* in the bigger, multiseat district elections than in the one-seat districts.[23] There are two reasons for this apparent paradox: candidates from one party can pool some of their expenses (activities designed to get out the vote, mailings, some advertisements, and so on), and it may be harder to pursue negative campaigning when there are several viable candidates on the ballot. The head-to-head combat of single-member districts appears to escalate the need for campaign spending.

- *Will full-representation voting systems be too confusing for voters?* No. Exit polls taken in Texas and elsewhere have demonstrated that voters understand the voting rules of alternative systems such as cumulative voting.[24] Full-representation systems are used in many American elections and in most other well-established democracies around the world. Voters in these elections have no trouble using them, as evidenced by the higher voter turnout rate seen in most nations that use a full-representation system. Some such systems are simple to describe; others sound more complicated when first described, but experience shows that voters quickly grasp and learn the new rules. An educational campaign instructing voters how to vote can also aid with the transition.

- *Will these systems undercut neighborhood representation?* No. With a full-representation system, you need a smaller percentage of votes to win, allowing candidates to target their campaigning to certain parts of the city, if they wish. In Cambridge, Massachusetts, where choice voting is used to elect their city council, five out of nine winning candidates typically have a core base of support in specific neighborhoods. Most neighborhoods consistently elect a representative from their area, as geography is often a factor in how some people vote. In Japan, local elections use limited voting for most city elections, and neighborhoods are also quite well represented, as neighborhood associations are often the most significant political players at that level of election.

- *Does advocacy of full representation undercut voting rights strategies using single-seat districts?* No. A full-representation system can clearly co-exist with a single-member district as a voting rights remedy. Some cities such as Peoria combine the approaches (districts with cumulative voting) in the same election. In states such as Texas, North Carolina, and Alabama, where many jurisdictions have adopted limited voting or cumulative voting, other localities have moved to single-seat districts. At the very least, a full-representation system is a sensible back-up option if a single-seat district cannot be drawn because of geographic dispersion of the minority constituency, or judicial or legislative opposition.

Reapportionment and Redistricting

The rising interest in alternative voting systems obviously is not occurring in a vacuum. Voting Rights Act provisions on redistricting have divided and preoccupied the Supreme Court more than any other issue for the past ten years. The Court has heard arguments on cases involving voting rights and redistricting each term since its *Shaw v. Reno* ruling in 1993, often producing bitterly contested five-to-four rulings that have had the general (if still poorly defined) impact of limiting to what degree a state can use race in drawing legislative district lines. In a bid to make some lemonade out of the Supreme Court's lemons, some long-time voting rights experts have reluctantly outlined the rationalization for accepting Shaw's "bizarre-shape" test over *Miller's* "dominant-purpose" test as the lesser of two evils.[25]

The traditional standard used by the courts to determine voting rights standing has been to demonstrate the ability to draw a majority-minority district; it is a standard that has always plagued geographically dispersed minorities like APAs. But in a 1998 *Harvard Civil Rights-Civil Liberties Law Review* article, Steven Mulroy, a Department of Justice civil rights attorney, argued for another yardstick,[26] proposing that Voting Rights Act liability be established and alternative remedies obtained even where the plaintiff cannot draw a compact majority-minority district but can demonstrate sufficient numbers to reach the victory threshold of viability (the Droop threshold) necessary for an alternative voting system. Using Mulroy's legal approach would still allow drawing majority-minority districts if the intervention proved to be the most effective. But it would also allow use of other interventions such as full representation if a majority-minority district cannot be drawn because of geographic dispersion of the targeted constituency or political or judicial opposition. Thus Mulroy's approach is more comprehensive and a powerful tool in voting rights lawsuits, offering to dispersed minority groups like APAs a way out of a dilemma posed by the race-conscious imperative of the Voting Rights Act and the race-neutral limits of *Shaw v. Reno*.

But there can be pragmatic arguments for proportional systems quite apart from the legal battles over *Shaw*. As civil rights attorneys have discovered in more than fifty Texas jurisdictions with cumulative voting and in the more than two dozen counties and cities in North Carolina and Alabama that have settled with limited voting, a full-representation system is sometimes a good fit with local conditions. Perhaps the minority community is more geographically dispersed than necessary for a single-seat district plan, as with the APA communities in New York City, Los Angeles, and San Francisco, where majority-minority districts have utterly failed to adequately represent APAs, electing only one APA out of seventy-seven local government seats. Perhaps a small jurisdiction wants to avoid redistricting every decade. In some multiracial communities, small and large, a citywide full-representation plan is the easiest way for racial minorities to elect representation without the pitfalls of gerrymandering and perennial lawsuits.

Local government is an obvious place for considering full-representation plans; the calculation of what it takes to win representation is quite straightforward. Redistricting and reapportionment, especially in racially diverse and polyglot cities such as Los Angeles, New York City, and San Francisco, pose several vexing questions. Should single-seat districts continue to be the preferred voting rights remedy, even if such a district produces electoral success for certain minority groups at the expense of other minority groups? Conversely, if it can be demonstrated that a multiseat full-representation system will do a better job than single-seat districts at giving political representation to all racial minority groups in a given locality, isn't there a voting rights imperative that such schemes be used? Knowing what we now know about the ineffectiveness of single-seat districts for yielding electoral success to APA voters in New York City, Los Angeles, San Francisco, and elsewhere, isn't it time for the voting rights community to explore alternative voting systems that are fair to everyone?

Given the new and vague rules established by the courts for drawing single-seat districts, full-representation voting systems show great promise for producing the most equitable solution for all.

Appendix: A Lexicon of Full-Representation Voting Systems

Full representation, also known as proportional representation, is a principle rather than a specific voting system. The principle is that groupings of like-minded voters should win representation in proportion to their voting strength. Certain voting systems fulfill this principle more than others, and various full-representation systems exist. The details of the system matter, but the key point is that all voters are empowered to mobilize and win their fair share of representation.

There are partisan and nonpartisan forms; more than two hundred localities in the United States use one of three nonpartisan systems: cumulative voting, limited voting, or choice voting. Candidates are elected at-large or in multiseat districts (constituencies electing more than one representative). Limited voting, cumulative voting, and choice voting are based on voting for candidates (not parties) and already are used in local elections in the United States.

Limited voting: a system where voters either cast fewer votes than the number of seats or political parties nominate fewer candidates than there are seats. The greater the difference between the number of seats and the number of votes, the greater the opportunity for minority representation. Versions of limited voting are used in Washington, D.C.; Philadelphia; Hartford, Connecticut; and numerous local jurisdictions. It has been used to resolve at least twenty-five voting rights cases. Limited voting with one vote—the method fairest to those in the minority—is used for nearly all municipal elections in Japan.

Example: in a race to elect five candidates, voters could be limited to one or two votes. The highest vote-getters (simple plurality)—that is, the five candidates with the most votes—win.

Cumulative voting: a system where voters cast as many votes as there are seats to be elected, but unlike a traditional at-large system voters are not limited to giving only one vote to a candidate. Instead, they can cast multiple votes for one or more candidates. In a five-seat race, a voter can give all five of her votes to one candidate, or three votes to one candidate and two votes to another candidate, and so on. She can cumulate, or "spend," her votes however she wishes.

Cumulative voting was used to elect the Illinois state legislature from 1870 to 1980. In recent years, it has been used to resolve voting rights cases for city council elections in numerous jurisdictions in Texas, Illinois, New Mexico, South Dakota, and elsewhere.

Example: in a race to elect five candidates, voters can cast one vote for five candidates, five votes for one candidate, or a combination in between. The five highest vote-getters (simple plurality) win.

Choice voting: the fairest candidate-based full-representation system, also known as "single transferable vote" and "preference voting." Choice voting is the most common full-representation system found in other English-speaking nations. Each voter has one vote but can rank as few or as many candidates as he wishes in order of preference (1, 2, 3, 4, and so on). Ballots are counted like a series of runoffs, eliminating candidates with the least support. Candidates win by reaching a victory threshold roughly equal to the number of votes divided by the number of seats. The ranked ballots facilitate coalition building and allow candidates to run without fear of being a spoiler, that is, splitting the vote.

Choice voting is used for city council and school board elections in Cambridge, Massachusetts (since 1941), where the city council has consistently had African American representation since the 1950s. Choice voting has also been used for local school board elections in New York City, where it has consistently produced a high rate of representation for African Americans, Latinos, and APAs (higher than the district elections used for city council and other offices). Choice voting was used until the 1950s in Cincinnati, Cleveland, New York City, and other American cities and resulted in fair racial, ethnic, and partisan representation. The Republic of Ireland and Australia use choice voting for national legislative elections and have done so for decades.

In addition, varieties of the proportional system are used in most well-established democracies; of the thirty-seven major democracies with a high Freedom House human rights rating and a population of more than two million people, only two—the United States and Canada—use exclusively a winner-take-all system for national elections.

Notes

1. Full representation voting systems such as cumulative voting, limited voting, and choice voting (also known as the "single transferable vote") are designed to create more opportunity for the electoral viability of voting minorities than the traditional, winner-take-all, at-large method of election, even though they do not involve use of single-member districts. Each such system features elections held jurisdictionwide ("multiseat" or at-large), without carving up the jurisdiction into subdistricts. However, unlike the traditional at-large system, these three systems employ special voting rules designed to enhance the ability of minority voting blocs to obtain representation. See Still, E. "Alternatives to Single-Member Districts." In C. Davidson (ed.), *Minority Vote Dilution.* Washington, D.C.: Howard University Press, 1984.

2. Followwill, R. "Cumulative Voting." *Amarillo Globe-News,* Aug. 1, 1999.

3. Bill Lann Lee, letter to Eric Proshansky, assistant corporation counsel, City of New York, Feb. 4, 1999.

4. See Guinier, L. "The Representation of Minority Interests: The Question of Single-Member Districts." 14 *Cardozo L. Rev.* 1135, 1137 (1993); "No Two Seats: The Elusive Quest for Political Equality." 77 *Va. L. Rev.* 1413 (1991); "The Triumph of Tokenism: The Voting Rights Act and the Theory of Black Electoral Success." 89 *Mich. L. Rev.* 1077 (1991).

5. *Shaw* v. *Reno,* 509 U.S. 630 (1993); *Miller* v. *Johnson,* 115 S.Ct. 2475 (1995); *Vera* v. *Bush,* 116 S.Ct. 1941 (1996); *Shaw* v. *Hunt,* 116 S.Ct. 1894 (1996); *Abrams* v. *Johnson,* 117 S.Ct. 1925 (1997).

6. A single-member (or single-seat) district, the traditional voting rights remedy, carves up a jurisdiction into geographic boundaries within which a single representative is elected by the voters within that geographic area to represent the area. It contrasts with a multimember (or multiseat) district, a geographic area from which more than one representative is elected; and an at-large system, in which no districts are used and voters from all over the jurisdiction may vote for multiple representatives.

7. See DeLeon, R., Blash, L., and Hill, S. "The Politics of Electoral Reform in San Francisco: Preference Voting Versus Districts Versus Plurality at-Large." Paper presented at the 1997 Annual Meeting of the Western Political Science Association, Tucson, Ariz., Mar. 13–15, 1997.

8. See, for example, Anderson, J. "Go Back to the Drawing Board to Make More Votes Count." *Christian Science Monitor,* Jan. 12, 1996, p. 18; Raspberry, W. "The Balkanization of America." *Washington Post,* July 7, 1995, op-ed page; "A Route to Fairer Voting." *USA Today,* June 30, 1995, sec. 1A, p. 12; Applebome, P. "Guinier Ideas, Once Seen as Odd, Now Get Serious Study." *New York Times,* Apr. 3, 1994, sec. 1A, p. 9.

9. The threshold of representation for proportional representation can be determined by one of two formulas. The first is called the Hare threshold and is determined by dividing the number of contested seats into the number of votes cast:

$$\frac{\text{Total number of votes cast}}{\text{Number of contested seats}}$$

The second is called the Droop threshold and is determined by dividing the number of contested seats plus one into the number of votes cast plus one more vote:

$$\frac{\text{Total number of votes cast} + 1}{\text{Number of contested seats} + 1}$$

Qualitatively, the Droop threshold is equal to the least number of votes a candidate needs to win such that, when all seats are filled, there are not enough votes left over to elect another candidate.

10. Letters to Department of Justice from Asian American Legal Defense and Education Fund, Sept. 1998–Feb. 1999.

11. Choice voting is a proportional-representation voting system also known as single transferable vote and preference voting. Each voter is allowed (but not required) to rank her or his favorite candidates in order of choice, 1, 2, 3, and so on. Ballots are counted like a series of runoff elections, and the victory threshold is determined by use of the aforementioned Hare or Droop threshold. Typically, choice voting requires a far smaller percentage of the vote to win a seat. In the New York City school board elections, a winning candidate needs just 10 percent of the vote to win one seat.

12. As usual, there were unfortunate—and unnecessary—problems with the type of ballot count used for choice voting elections in New York City. New York persists in counting these ballots by hand, rather than automating and computerizing the process, as Cambridge, Massachusetts, has done.

13. Letters to Department of Justice from Asian American Legal Defense and Education Fund, Sept. 1998–Feb. 1999.

14. The Droop threshold (not the Hare threshold) is used in New York City for community school board elections.

15. Engstrom, R. L. "Modified Multi-Seat Election Systems as Remedies for Minority Vote Dilution." 21 *Stetson L. Rev.* 743, 750 (1992); Engstrom, R., Taebel, D. A., and Cole, R. L. "Cumulative Voting as a Remedy for Minority Vote Dilution: The Case of Alamogordo." *Journal of Law and Politics,* Spring 1989, 5, 469–497; Engstrom, R., and Barrilleaux, C. "Native Americans and Cumulative Voting: The Sisseton-Wahpeton Sioux." *Social Science Quarterly,* 1991, 72, pp. 388, 391–392; Brischetto, R., and Engstrom, R. "Cumulative Voting and Latino Representation: Exit Surveys in Fifteen Texas Communities." Social Science Quarterly, 1997, 78(4).

16. Brockington, D., Donovan, T., Bowler, S., and Brischetto, R. "Minority Representation under Limited and Cumulative Voting." *Journal of Politics,* Nov. 1998, 60, 1108–1125.

17. Gray, J. *Winning Fair Representation in At-Large Elections: Cumulative Voting and Limited Voting in Alabama Local Elections.* Takoma Park, Md.: Southern Regional Council and Center for Voting and Democracy, 1999.

18. Pildes, R. H., and Donoghue, K. A. "Cumulative Voting in the United States." University of Chicago Legal Forum, 1995, 241–313.

19. "Voting age population" rather than "registered voters" is generally used in voting rights cases, because it is less open to quick fluctuation and a more accurate count of the number of eligible voters who choose to participate or not. But differentials in registered voters obviously have an impact and must be factored in when determining electoral viability.

20. Using the Droop threshold {[1/(number of seats + 1)] + 1 vote}, three seats produce a representation threshold of 25 percent plus one more vote.

21. Using the Droop threshold, five seats produce a representation threshold of 16.67 percent plus one more vote.

22. Wong, S. "District Elections: Who Benefits?" *Asian Week,* Jan. 18, 2001. Wong estimated the Asian population in 2000 to be more like 40 percent of San Francisco.

23. "Bigger Districts Don't Mean More Expensive Campaigns." Takoma Park, Md.: Center for Voting and Democracy, Money and Elections, 1996. (www.fairvote.org/money/seats_costs.htm)

24. Brischetto and Engstrom (1997); Engstrom, R. L., and Brischetto, R. R. "Is Cumulative Voting Too Complex? Evidence from Exit Polls." *Stetson Law Review,* Winter 1998, 27, 813–834.

25. Karlan, P. S. "The Fire Next Time: Reapportionment After the 2000 Census." *Stanford Law Review*, Feb. 1998, *50*, 729–763.

26. Mulroy, S. J. "The Way Out: A Legal Standard for Imposing Alternative Electoral Systems as Voting Rights Remedies." *Harvard Civil Rights-Civil Liberties Law Review*, 1998, *33*, 333.

27. See Reynolds, A., and Reilly, B. *The International IDEA Handbook of Electoral System Design.* Stockholm: Institute for Democracy and Electoral Assistance, 1997.

Steven Hill is the Center for Voting and Democracy's senior analyst, and author of Fixing Elections.

Robert Richie is executive director of the Center for Voting and Democracy (www. fairvote.org). He is coauthor with Steven Hill of Reflecting All of Us.

Taking Democracy to Scale: Creating a Town Hall Meeting for the Twenty-First Century

Carolyn J. Lukensmeyer, Steve Brigham

Over the last decade we have watched democracy surge and ebb around the world. With its firm commitment to strengthening democratic movements, the United States has encouraged, directly assisted in, and even led many democratization efforts. Yet to maintain a credible leadership role, we must acknowledge that our own democracy has much room for improvement. A healthy democracy depends on the ability of citizens[1] to affect the public policies that deeply influence their lives, and ours does not currently allow citizens their rightful voice in decision making. Special-interest groups have captured the processes for democratic input. They have skewed the agenda toward extreme positions and alienated many citizens who would tend toward a middle ground.

For this reason and many others, citizens distrust their elected officials, don't vote, and are deeply cynical about government. Conversely, policy makers believe citizens hold fast to uninformed opinions and operate from self-interest. In the end, the gap between people and the decision-making processes that affect their lives continues to widen. Despite this state of affairs, our experience working with citizens in all regions of the country leaves us confident that people want to get involved and change things for the better.

Unfortunately, the traditional methods our government has used for involving citizens give little inspiration for the public to reinvest in civic life. Public hearings and typical town hall meetings are not a meaningful way for citizens to engage in governance and to have an impact on decision making. They are speaker-focused, with experts simply delivering information or responding to questions. Little learning occurs, for citizens or decision makers, because airing individual concerns too often devolves into repetitive ax grinding, grandstanding, or even a shouting match between various stakeholders. In the end, decision makers don't know which points of view have the most salience for

We wish to thank Wendy Jacobson, Joe Goldman, Lars Torres, and Liz White for their significant contributions to this article.

various groups because there has been no authentic, informed exchange of opinion and no opportunity to build a true consensus.

In short, our usual strategies for gathering input do not engage and sustain citizen interest or generate much useful information for decision makers. As a result, they do little to reinvigorate and expand participation in civic life. Further, in this climate of high distrust between citizens and their government, it is not enough to simply inform citizens. A healthy democracy requires that citizens be able to have an impact on the public decisions and governance processes that most affect them.

We began to imagine the outlines of a response to this situation as we interviewed a broad spectrum of citizens and public officials. How could we help decision makers go beyond polling to connect quickly and authentically with citizen voices? How could we tap into the value of informal citizen conversation and make sure the wisdom was heard and citizen voices respected? How could we deepen the relationship between decision makers and the public so that citizens could have a tangible impact on policy making and resource planning? The 21st Century Town Meeting™ was created to answer these questions.[2] It was created to meet the needs of citizens *and* decision makers—to meet the needs of our democracy.

Decision makers who want to understand and act on the collective wisdom of their constituency are well served by the aggregate power of a large number of citizen voices. Citizens who want to be heard by decision makers desire meaningful in-depth dialogue and tend to thrive in a small-scale setting. The 21st Century Town Meeting serves both of these needs through using the latest information technology. Strategically designed, the model enables thousands of citizens to simultaneously participate in intimate, face-to-face deliberation and contribute to the collective wisdom of a very large group. By engaging a large, demographically representative group in public deliberation, the 21st Century Town Meeting ensures that (1) all voices are at the table (those of the general public and of key stakeholders), (2) the voice of the public gets the attention of decision makers and the media, and (3) a substantial segment of the public supports the results of the forum and has a stake in its implementation.

The 21st Century Town Meeting revives this country's strongly held belief that naturally occurring conversation about important public issues has significant value. It revises the current iteration of the town hall meeting to produce citizen deliberation that is well informed, synthesized, and directly connected to real opportunity for action. This model has proven successful in engaging thousands of citizens around the country in a deliberative process having a real influence on regional planning, local budget decisions, and national policy development. The 21st Century Town Meeting brings large-scale deliberation, with direct links to decision makers, to the continuum of efforts in the citizen engagement field.

The true potential of this model can best be seen in its most recent and largest-scale implementation: a town hall meeting in New York City that drew more than forty-three hundred people to deliberate over plans for reconstruction of the World Trade Center site. The citizen input gathered at "Listening to the City" has had continuing and significant influence on the plans for rebuilding the World Trade Center and creating a permanent memorial. This article describes the 21st Century Town Meeting model (its innovative elements, theoretical base, and methodology), demonstrates its impact using Listening to the City as a case study, highlights other applications for the model, and frames it among the range of important strategies for reengaging citizens in our democracy.

What Is a 21st Century Town Meeting?

The 21st Century Town Meeting has been in development by the nonprofit organization America*Speaks* since 1995. This model innovatively integrates several important technologies and methods to enable thousands of citizens to come together and develop an action-ready slate of recommendations about complicated public issues, all in one day. These are the technologies and methods:

• *Small-group dialogue.* Demographically diverse groups of ten to twelve participants come together with the support of a trained facilitator for in-depth discussion of values and key aspects of the issue under consideration. The size of the group creates a safe space for participants to learn from one another, react to ideas, use the materials provided to inform their opinion, and ultimately arrive at a collective view that represents the best integration of individual perspectives.

• *Networked computers.* Computers serve as electronic flipcharts, creating an instant record of the ideas generated at tables and ensuring that all voices are heard and no idea is lost. Through a wireless network, they transmit data to a central computer, setting the stage for distillation of themes from every table and for the voting process.

• *Theming.* Members of a "theme team" read electronic comments from all the tables in real time and distill them into key themes or messages. The themes are then presented back to the entire room so participants can respond to and vote on them.

• *Electronic keypads.* Each participant in a 21st Century Town Meeting has a wireless keypad for voting on issues and measuring his or her position with respect to other participants. Keypads also are used to establish the demographics of the event so that participants get a sense of the larger group of which they are a part. Keypad voting yields volumes of demographically sortable data that can be of great value to decision makers, as well as to the media as they develop the story. Keypad voting creates transparency during the meeting and enables participants to see that their voices are being heard.

• *Large video screens.* Large screens project data, themes, and information in real time to the entire gathering. When themes (and the corresponding level of support in the room) are projected on the screens, thousands of people get instant feedback on how the results of discussion at their table fit with what happened at other tables. With large screens, individuals see the will of the whole as it gradually develops over the course of the day.

Using technology to gather, distill, and project themes and concerns allows a 21st Century Town Meeting to move back and forth between intimate small-group dialogue and the collective work of thousands of people. This back-and-forth between the small-scale and large-scale dialogues can occur as many times as needed to develop recommendations on which decision makers can take action.

What does a 21st Century Town Meeting actually look like from start to finish? The day begins with a welcome from sponsors, and brief opening comments from key political leaders to set the context for the issues under discussion. Participants begin by answering a series of demographic questions using keypad polling, both to get oriented to the technology and to find out who is in the room, by age, gender, race, income, geography, and other criteria relevant to the issue being discussed. Before any deliberation on key content, there is a values-based discussion to allow participants to learn what is important to them regarding the issues at hand. The values identified by participants lay the foundation for the next four to five hours of discussion on key issues. As already described, in each segment of the agenda discussion begins at individual tables, is themed in real time, and is then presented back to the whole for clarification and modification, and finally for voting. The last twenty or twenty-five minutes are to evaluate the day, review next steps, and allow time for decision makers to comment on what they have heard from participants. A report summarizing the outcomes of the day is quickly developed, reproduced, and distributed to participants, sponsors, and officials as they leave. By the end of the day, decision makers and citizens have heard the collective wisdom of a large, demographically representative cross-section of the public. Because decision makers have participated in the event and agreed to act on the recommendations in some way, the voices that come together at a 21st Century Town Meeting have a lasting impact.

The Theory and Methodology of the Model

The 21st Century Town Meeting is more than a single event. It is an integrated process of citizen, stakeholder, and decision-maker engagement over the course of many months. Seven elements (some discrete and some ongoing through the life of the project) make up the theoretical base and methodology of the model.

Selecting an Issue That Affects Policy and Resources for the Common Good. Citizen deliberation can affect the terms and outcome of a debate, the shape and content of policy enacted, or how dollars are allocated in a budget.

But whatever the subject matter, disgruntled and disenfranchised citizens are more likely to engage in the political process if they believe they are involved in something with significant impact. The issue selection process should ensure the potential for impact in the real world in a reasonable time frame. The work should be linked to governance processes that already exist so that follow-up action can come quickly. In the end, the processes that govern how the public's work is done must be affected.

Developing the Strategy. The life of a key public issue constantly shifts and evolves. The issue selected for a 21st Century Town Meeting should be continuously analyzed in both the political and the communications contexts. Who are the key decision makers, stakeholders, and communities, and what is the nature of their stake in the issue? How would a deliberation build on previous activity? When would a deliberation be most salient?

Building Credibility with Citizens and Decision Makers. Citizen deliberation has the capacity for significant impact if there is a meaningful, transparent link to an appropriate decision-making process and decision makers. Decision makers must be present, listening, and publicly committed to taking outcomes into consideration. Partisanship and bias must be absent from the planning and execution of events, participant mix, and discussion materials.

Ensuring Diverse Participation. Although the level of civic engagement in general is low, it is lowest among a critical group: unorganized, unaffiliated citizens. Participant outreach must ensure a diverse mix of citizens, with a specific commitment to reaching those who are unorganized and unaffiliated. A target should be set for the number of participants sufficient to demonstrate that the community is active and cares about the issue, and to command the attention of decision makers and the media.

Creating Safe Public Space. The event must be designed to consistently seek fair and productive dialogue and create a level playing field on which individual citizen voices are equal to those representing established interests. There must be ample time for extensive small-group discussion, balanced by time for large-group synthesis and recommendations. Technology can be used to make sure everyone is heard and no strongly held idea is lost.

Supporting Informed Dialogue. Important conversations about public issues occur naturally among ordinary citizens and can be significantly enhanced by infusing high-quality information. To counter the perception that citizens hold uninformed views, educational material should offer sufficient context and history on the issues, be neutral and fair to all perspectives, leave room for citizens to create new options, and have credibility with all audiences.

Sustaining and Institutionalizing Citizen Voice. One town meeting does not make a vital public participation process. The issues selected and the overall strategy developed must incorporate ways to seed and track both systemic change among decision makers and a renewed sense of agency among participants. There must be an avenue by which a citizen can continue to pursue the issue.

Putting this conceptual framework into action, the 21st Century Town Meeting offers a model for democratic deliberation that is practical, meets needs that are strongly felt by citizens and government officials, and produces compelling recommendations on public policy in a time frame that aligns with a modern cycle of governance and the time demands of the media. A 21st Century Town Meeting can demonstrate the value for governments of including citizens in the decisions that have an impact on their lives; it can position the citizen as a central player in governance and urge a new way of thinking about public dialogue, both in the physical place where it is held and in the social and emotional space created to support it. All of this is part of a process America*Speaks* calls "Taking Democracy to Scale."™

Taking Democracy to Scale: A Case Study of Listening to the City

On July 20, 2002, more than forty-three hundred citizens from New York City and the surrounding area came together for the largest face-to-face town hall meeting ever held. Using the 21st Century Town Meeting model, these citizens deliberated over specific options for redeveloping the World Trade Center site and considered strategies for helping people rebuild their lives in the aftermath of September 11. As a direct result of their deliberation, the participants secured commitment from top officials that development plans would be revised along the lines they suggested. Following the meeting, the governor of New York reiterated the citizens' directives to go back to the drawing board on site design options, develop mixed-use plans, reduce the density of the site, and find new solutions to the issue of commercial space. Three months later, the voices of these citizens were still being heeded as new decisions were made about redeveloping Ground Zero.

Listening to the City was an extraordinary feat of planning, coalition building, staffing, and large-scale application of information technologies. In the end, its success proves unequivocally that the model works. This description of the planning and execution of Listening to the City demonstrates how the 21st Century Town Meeting model is democracy in action.

A Coalition Is Built

A few months after the September 11 attacks, the Civic Alliance to Rebuild Downtown New York (a coalition of more than eighty-five business, labor, community, and civic groups) was convened. The alliance is a broad umbrella for civic planning and advocacy efforts in support of rebuilding lower Manhattan; it seeks to ensure that a vigorous and productive public discussion takes place. The alliance's principal partners (the Regional Plan Association, NYU/Robert F. Wagner Graduate School, New School University, and the Pratt Institute Center for Community and Environmental Development) invited America*Speaks* to design a series of public conversations about the city's needs in the wake of the destruction of the World Trade Center. The first, held on February 7, 2002, brought more than 650 people from throughout the metropolitan area together with experts and regional leaders to discuss the vision and principles that should inform the rebuilding process.

Following this success, the alliance forged a formal partnership with the Lower Manhattan Development Corporation (LMDC) and the Port Authority of New York and New Jersey (Port Authority) and began planning a second public deliberation, to be held five months later for as many as five thousand citizens. An executive team (composed of leaders from America*Speaks* and the principal partners) went to work determining strategy, developing budgets, hiring outside consultants for a range of tasks (recruitment, communications and public relations, event management, registration), and guiding project leaders and staff.

Outreach Begins

A project of this magnitude required highly skilled outreach on a massive scale. A crack team was pulled together of more than a dozen full-time and part-time field organizers who lived in or had worked extensively within the communities in which they were recruiting participants. The outreach team developed strong relationships within each targeted community and secured assistance and commitment from organizations and leaders to support the event and assist in recruiting. Registrations began to flow in during the first half of June at a rate of about three hundred per week. After the Fourth of July weekend, they arrived at a rate of about three hundred to four hundred per day. As the rolls grew, the outreach team identified which demographic and geographic populations were underrepresented. In the last weeks, ads ran in publications targeted to communities where registration was low, and there was additional street outreach.

Key Decision Makers and the Media Get on Board

From the beginning, Listening to the City was designed in conjunction with New York's official process for redevelopment of Ground Zero. The two principal decision-making stakeholders were the LMDC, created and charged by the governor with the overall planning and revitalization process; and the Port Authority, the owner of the World Trade Center site and the party responsible for transportation infrastructure and management of port commerce facilities and services. The LMDC played an active role in Listening to the City, not only as a significant financial sponsor but also in planning content. The Port Authority played a quietly supportive role until the final weeks, when it became a more visible partner. Importantly, both LMDC and the Port Authority endorsed and partially financed the event; this strengthened confidence that the voices and collective judgment of the participants would be heard by those with decision-making authority.

Media interest in Listening to the City—critical to securing participation as well as legitimacy in the public eye—emerged gradually. In the first couple of months, coverage was slow. Outreach efforts focused on engaging neighborhood newspapers and local radio stations, and as momentum built the major media began to take an interest. In the end, more than two hundred media outlets—including all of the major networks; dozens of major newspaper dailies from around the country; and media from across Canada, Europe, and Asia—covered the event.

The Critical Staff Structure Comes Together

Managing a town meeting of forty-three hundred required a crew of about one thousand volunteers and staff, including hundreds who were specially trained and selected for four functional areas fundamental to the success of the event:

• *Table facilitators* with a strong background in small-group facilitation as well as the experience and confidence to work an intensive day-long program were assigned to each of the five hundred tables. The key tenets of a 21st Century Town Meeting (creating a safe space for real dialogue, equalizing participants, ensuring responsiveness to all viewpoints) could not be upheld without productive table deliberation, for which skilled facilitation is critical. More than eight hundred individuals volunteered to be table facilitators, willing to travel and participate at their own expense. In the end, the table facilitators represented all fifty states plus Canada, the United Kingdom, Australia, South Africa, Colombia, and Denmark—a testament to the power of the event.

• *Theme team members* (as noted earlier) read ideas that were generated at the tables and sent to them through a wireless network. They distilled the comments into key themes or messages and presented the themes back to the room to validate what was discussed and allow further refinements. The theme team is the component of the model that makes the meeting immediately responsive to citizen views and input; it enables final recommendations for action to go directly to decision makers.

• *Issue experts* answered participants' substantive questions. The 21st Century Town Meeting's ability to take a large number of citizens through complex, multifaceted issue deliberation derives from the model's emphasis on using meticulously crafted informational material that is politically neutral, highly substantive, and accessible. The availability of issue experts during this event further served the goal of maintaining high-level issue discussion.

• *Constituency service representatives* from city, state, and federal agencies linked to the rebuilding process were stationed outside the room to answer questions not pertinent to the day's agenda. By helping participants with their concerns, these volunteers supported the model's emphasis on creating a safe space for productive dialogue. Their work helped keep table discussions on task, making sure the group could get through a complex agenda in a short time.

In addition to these groups, hundreds of volunteers took on other tasks leading up to and during Listening to the City: calling all registrants to remind them of the meeting time and give them last-minute details; stuffing five thousand participant folders with guides, worksheets, and other background materials and dropping additional printed materials on all five hundred tables; registering participants on site; serving as greeters and escorts; managing meal distribution; delivering any printed material missing at an individual table; helping people with special needs such as grief counseling; troubleshooting, supporting facilitation at the tables, answering questions, obtaining material, and finding on-site experts when needed for consultation; and handling software, hardware, or computer operation questions.

The Day Arrives

Once forty-three hundred participants were in their seats and had answered demographic questions about themselves on their wireless keypads, everyone saw that the room looked much like a microcosm of the New York region. There were roughly equal numbers of men and women, with a good mix of age groups, except for youth (who, as it turns out, had much greater representation in the two-week online dialogue that followed the event). Racial diversity did not match the regional census precisely but was still notable, with 14 percent of participants identifying themselves as "mixed racial heritage" or "other," 12 percent Asian, 10 percent Hispanic, 7 percent African American, and 67 percent Caucasian.[3] Forty-six percent of the participants were from Manhattan; 32 percent from the other four boroughs; and 22 percent from New York State, New Jersey, and Connecticut, or any other location in the United States or abroad. There was also socioeconomic diversity: 17 percent of participants reported household income at or below $25,000, while 13 percent were at or above $150,000. Finally, there was solid representation by those with a personal connection to the events of September 11. Roughly one in five identified themselves as survivors of the attack, more than 40 percent worked in lower Manhattan, and more than 20 percent lived there.

Listening to the City began with values discussions, which identified shared hopes among the forty-three hundred participants. On the basis of these collective values, the two issue discussions that followed assessed the six site options and developed a specific agenda for revitalizing the downtown and surrounding areas. On the first issue, participants voiced strong objections to elements of all six site options. More than a third said the proposals were not ambitious enough. Most favored more open space and a memorial that is inspirational, serene, and integrated into the plan for the entire site. In terms of revitalization directives, citizens expressed a desire for affordable and middle-income housing for all ages, and to see lower Manhattan become a more diverse, livelier community. They advised expanding transit service (including bringing commuter trains directly downtown and affording better access to nearby neighborhoods such as Chinatown) as well as improving existing systems and reducing traffic congestion. Participants also wanted more business diversity without diluting the character of Lower Manhattan as a financial district. Finally, they urged creation of job and training programs, particularly for those most affected by the terrorist attack.

At the close of Listening to the City, representatives from LMDC, the Port Authority, and the mayor's office confirmed that the day's events would have a profound impact on the rebuilding process. They agreed to go back to the drawing board, develop mixed-use plans, reduce the density of the site, and find new solutions to resolve the main leaseholder's rights. As participants and decision makers left the hall, they received a written report summarizing the key findings and recommendations.

Following the event, an online dialogue brought an additional 818 people into the deliberation through twenty-six small discussion groups that "met" over the next two weeks. The online dialogue fostered thoughtful interaction by (1) engaging participants in the discussion when it was convenient to them; (2) allowing people to explore the issues more thoroughly by extending the time frame; and (3) permitting participants to monitor discussion in all the other groups, and use this information to develop their own views more fully. In two weeks, as many as ten thousand messages were exchanged; satisfaction with the online dialogue was consistent with the experiences of the "in person" participants. Interestingly, almost half of the online deliberators reported it was their first experience with such dialogue. In the end, messages from the online dialogue confirmed and added value to the work undertaken by the original group.

The Recommendations Take Hold

A few weeks after Listening to the City, LMDC announced that it would open the planning process to six new design teams from around the world. Of the $21 billion in federal money promised to New York City, $4.55 billion was earmarked for a Lower Manhattan transit hub, a key recommendation from the meeting. The Port Authority also expressed real willingness to move commercial development from Ground Zero to other locations in lower Manhattan. Three months after Listening to the City, officials took further action that was directly responsive to citizen recommendations. They agreed to reduce by 40 percent the amount of commercial space that must be included in the site designs and allow expansion of hotel and retail space.

Did Listening to the City Take Democracy to Scale?

The Listening to the City event met or exceeded expectations in terms of participation; smooth implementation; and the strength, clarity, and consistency of the citizenry's voice that emerged. But did it actually take democracy to scale? Did it create a process by which a significant number of citizens had a discernible impact on policy making and governance, and lay the groundwork for sustained civic involvement among its participants?

We think the answer to these questions is yes. Listening to the City brought thousands of unaffiliated citizens together to deliberate in a safe and neutral space. The event supported informed dialogue and confirmed citizens' ability to wrestle with complicated issues and come to cogent and realistic recommendations. The finely orchestrated combination of facilitated face-to-face dialogue, massive information processing, and instant communication gave participants the opportunity to be heard by an intimate group as well as by thousands, including those making the decisions. The active participation of key stakeholders and their public commitment to change meant the event was openly and meaningfully linked to a decision-making process. Since that process was under way but still in an early stage, it was ripe for input. In the end, citizens' voices were heard, and their recommendations were heeded.

Other Applications for This Methodology

Potential applications for a 21st Century Town Meeting are numerous, but the America*Speaks* experience demonstrates that there are three kinds of public work (whether local, regional, or national in scope) that may be most appropriate for this methodology: planning, resource allocation, and policy formulation.

Planning. City, state, and regional planning efforts are complex enterprises involving weighing and prioritizing a range of substantive issues (from economic development to the environment, from housing to education), while balancing trade-offs between short-term and long-term investments. The 21st Century Town Meeting can take a large group of people through such a planning maze. The model's carefully developed participant guides and dialogue questions combine with the instant voting technology and theming capacity to enable participants to rank-order choices against a set of agreed-upon criteria and values. The model is well-suited to large-scale planning deliberation.

In January 2002, in Hamilton County, Ohio, America*Speaks* facilitated a 21st Century Town Meeting that enabled more than one thousand citizens to comment on elements of a comprehensive regional development plan (the first in thirty-five years), ratify a regional vision, set priorities, and offer strategies for action. Citizens offered specific suggestions for taking action in four priority areas: ensuring economic prosperity, building collaborative decision making, embracing diversity and equity, and balancing development and the environment. Action teams were established to turn the citizens' suggestions into specific action steps.

Resource Allocation. A second juncture at which the methodology can be particularly useful is when there are significant resources to be allocated—when elected officials must establish budget priorities and make tough choices.

Public budgets have enormous bearing on the quality of people's daily lives. Yet because needs consistently outpace available resources, there are always winners and losers in budget decision making. The 21st Century Town Meeting model levels the playing field. No organized group can take over the deliberations; everyone who comes participates in the same agenda, and all voices are equal. The design of the event ensures that the outcomes of the day are the collective wisdom and judgment of everyone present. Applying this very public and highly transparent process to budget decision making increases the likelihood of resource allocation reflecting the common good rather than the priorities of the most vocal special interests. It also creates a natural constituency for the budget as it moves through the political process.

In November 1999, America*Speaks* worked with the Washington, D.C., mayor's office to hold a series of 21st Century Town Meetings to help set the District of Columbia's strategic priorities. The strategic priorities determine how local tax dollars are allocated. The largest of these meetings drew more than three thousand participants, and a Youth Summit brought together fourteen hundred young people aged fourteen to twenty-one. In the end, citizen input led to redirected spending priorities for FY2001 in a number of areas. Among other things, some $70 million was added to the education budget, $10 million in new funding was allocated to improving senior services, one thousand new drug treatment slots were financed, new neighborhood-based supermarkets were approved, and funds were allocated for continued neighborhood-based planning and participation in governance. Three years later, more than fifteen hundred D.C. citizens have remained involved in an intensive way in the strategic "neighborhood action" work going on throughout the city. The FY2003 budget allocates another $2 million toward sustaining citizen involvement.

America*Speaks* also worked with the mayor's office to develop a comprehensive governance process. Every two years, citizens help to create a strategic plan that drives development of the city's budget, performance contracts for city employees, and a public scorecard that measures how well the city lived up to its commitments.

Policy Formulation. The 21st Century Town Meeting is particularly appropriate when critical public policy decisions are pending: whenever the current landscape is up for grabs, or when a cross-section of the American public has a real stake in the issue, or when polling data indicate that citizens believe they can reach consensus even if partisan positioning means politicians cannot. A 21st Century Town Meeting is ideal for working through contentious terrain because the model equalizes the voices of all participants and follows a design that intentionally builds consensus by using values-based questions to arrive at concrete decisions. Difficult issues such as health care reform, whether or not to undertake unilateral military action, or gun control are examples of issues that would be well served in this format.

In 1997–98, the Pew Charitable Trusts' "Americans Discuss Social Security" project (ADSS) used a combination of 21st Century Town Meetings, video teleconferencing, and small-scale local forums to bring more than forty-five thousand citizens in all fifty states into direct conversation with policy makers in Washington about addressing problems facing the Social Security system. By the end of the project, ADSS demonstrated that Americans agreed on three specific reform options: collecting payroll taxes on earnings above the salary cap, reducing benefits for people with high retirement income, and permitting workers to direct a share of their Social Security contributions toward private investment.

Whether in the area of planning, resource allocation, or policy formulation, a 21st Century Town Meeting is a particularly desirable methodology whenever decision making on a local issue directly informs national policies—or, conversely, when local decision making is in need of policy making at the national level. For example, local communities around the country that serve as gateways to national parks face similar concerns related to sprawl, congestion, and cost and revenue sharing. A 21st Century Town Meeting (using satellite video teleconferencing technology) can efficiently facilitate simultaneous multisite information sharing and deliberation. Such interaction is likely to improve the quality of local discussion and also may quickly raise key issues to national attention, potentially securing helpful action from decision makers.

In considering applications for the 21st Century Town Meeting, availability of infrastructure and resources is always an important consideration. The methodology is labor-intensive and costly. Yet even though the cost of putting on a 21st Century Town Meeting is substantial, it is sure to be comparable to (if not even less than) what is routinely spent by politicians and elected officials on public opinion polls and public relations strategies. In addition, authentic engagement of the public on controversial issues can mitigate the likelihood of expensive controversy and delay later on. Unfortunately, financing a large-scale public deliberation will continue to seem too costly until this country establishes an ethic that real-time citizen engagement is as important as polling.

The Emerging Field of Deliberative Democracy

Across the country and around the world, deliberative democracy is emerging as an exciting field of practice. At the heart of this work is the firm belief that our broken governance processes can be fixed. Innovative organizations are experimenting with a variety of new and better ways for citizens to participate in government decision making and help resolve public problems. In scattered pockets, citizens are learning about issues and engaging with the diversity of their communities—and their voices are making a difference.

This emerging field shares a set of values. We believe that the diversity of a community must be engaged. We are committed to informed deliberation that lets all participants be heard. We know that face-to-face dialogue is an experience that can change people's lives. We believe that public deliberation can and should make a difference. At the same time, several critical differences distinguish the various models under development: the scale of engagement, the level of governance in which change is sought, the kind of issue being addressed, and the strategies for using the results of deliberation to create change. For example:

- Although America*Speaks* engages thousands of people at one time in its 21st Century Town Meetings, the Study Circles Resource Center engages multiple groups of twelve to eighteen people several times and then later brings all of the groups together.
- The Center for Deliberative Polling conducts dialogues among a statistically reliable random sample of up to six hundred participants and measures resulting opinion changes.
- The Public Conversations Project seeks to create change by building understanding between communities in conflict.
- The National Issues Forum produces reports to Congress that represent opinions generated through forums across the country.

The approaches in this emerging field are many and varied.

In a different vein, a handful of groups (such as Web Lab, e-thePeople, and Information Renaissance) are experimenting with asynchronous online dialogue, which can take place over multiple weeks and engage a large or small group of citizens in discussion of policy issues. The dialogue may include a roundtable that brings together issue experts, public officials, and advocacy groups, or it may be composed of small groups of unaffiliated citizens. These groups are advancing the field by testing the possibility of real, informed deliberation among citizens by way of the Internet.

All of these efforts (and this is not intended to be an exhaustive list) are building an emerging field of practice. We believe the America*Speaks* 21st Century Town Meeting brings unique value to the work. The size and demographic diversity of our meetings captures the imagination of the media and decision makers in a way that is difficult to achieve on a smaller scale. The size and diversity also create a significant constituency that can keep pressure on decision makers to follow through. Because the events are linked to existing governance processes, it is possible to ensure that actions taken are highly visible and that accountability can be maintained.

As the deliberative democracy field develops, it becomes increasingly important for us to further distinguish the available citizen engagement strategies—to understand their strengths and weaknesses, and be able to match them to local capacity and substance areas. We must find creative ways to coordinate and collaborate with each other so the field is defined by a shared mission to create a healthier democracy. We must ensure that the collective power of citizens' voices is an integral part of governance and decision making.

Into the Future

A nascent movement is afoot to give citizens their due voice in decision making—in short, to reinvent American democracy. The time has come for those who care about the values and spirit of democracy to take up the banner of this movement. We know our democracy is broken, but we also know the will is there to fix it. Over the past six months, America*Speaks* has partnered with more than twenty organizations to create the Deliberative Democracy Consortium. The consortium will bring the best models together to develop shared strategies to achieve a healthier democracy.

In the years ahead, the deliberative democracy movement faces three principal challenges. First, we must transform how Americans think about themselves as citizens—how they conceptualize their role, responsibility, and relationship to their government. In short, we must help Americans understand what it can mean to be a citizen. Second, we must develop the nationwide infrastructure that is needed for citizens to participate in governance at all levels. Such an infrastructure must include everything from public space for citizens to come together in their community to a national network of facilitators who can support ongoing dialogue. It must support recruitment of citizens to participate in public dialogue and make available adequate mechanisms to educate citizens about issues that are addressed. Third, and most important, this nationwide infrastructure must connect citizens to decision makers and cycles of governance and management.

We believe America*Speaks* can play an important role in this movement. As we look to the future, we challenge ourselves to find ways to sustain citizen participation over time. We will do more to make sure that our process adequately reaches out and gives voice to those who are most disempowered in their community. We will learn how to better institutionalize this work and build capacity within the community to maintain it.

We are hopeful for our democracy. The values are there, the strategies are there, the people are there. It is simply up to all of us to make it happen. *New York Daily News* columnist Pete Hamill was at Listening to the City and saw citizens working hard to do just that:

> We came to the vast hangar at the Javits Center expecting the worst. Put 5,000 New Yorkers in a room, charge them with planning a hunk of the New York Future, and the result would be a lunatic asylum. . . . None of that happened. . . . From 10 A.M. to 4 P.M. they were presented with basic issues about the rebuilding of those 16 gutted acres in lower Manhattan. At each table they debated in a sober, thoughtful, civil way. They voted, offered comments, and moved on to the next item on the agenda. . . . And because the process was an exercise in democracy, not demagoguery, no bellowing idiots grabbed microphones to perform for the TV cameras. . . . In this room, "I" had given way to "we." Yes, the assembly was boring to look at, too

serious, too grave, too well-mannered for standard TV presentation. And it was absolutely thrilling. . . . We have a word for what they were doing. The word is democracy.

Notes

1. Throughout this article, the term *citizen* is meant to be inclusive of citizens and noncitizen residents.

2. 21st Century Town Meeting is trademarked by America*Speaks,* a national nonprofit organization. For purposes of readability, the trademark symbol is used only at the first appearance of the term in this article.

3. Percentages add up to more than 100 because participants had the option of identifying themselves in more than one category.

Carolyn J. Lukensmeyer is founder and president of AmericaSpeaks.

Steve Brigham is chief operating officer of AmericaSpeaks.

The Vanishing Voter: Why Are the Voting Booths So Empty?

Thomas E. Patterson

The period from 1960 to 2000 marks the longest ebb in voter turnout in the nation's history. Turnout was nearly 65 percent in 1960 but fell in each of the five succeeding presidential elections. It rose by one percentage point in 1984 but then fell by three points in 1988. Although analysts viewed that drop with alarm, the warning bells really sounded in 1996, when more Americans stayed home than went to the polls on Election Day.

Less publicized but no less dramatic has been the decline in voting in other elections. Turnout in the 2002 midterm elections was 39 percent. Several decades ago, these elections drew half the adult population to the polls. Many states and communities have recently experienced a record low voting rate. Turnout has also fallen in primary elections; in congressional primaries it was nearly 35 percent in the 1970s, but a mere 18 percent in 2002.

Fewer voters are not the only sign of the public's waning interest in political campaigns. In 1960, 60 percent of the nation's television households had their sets on and tuned to the October presidential debates. In 2000, less than 30 percent were tuned in. Few Americans today pay even token tribute to a presidential election. In 1974, Congress established a fund to underwrite candidates' campaigns, financed by a check-off box on the personal income tax return that allowed citizens to assign one dollar (later raised to three) of their tax liability to the fund. Initially, one in three taxpayers checked the box. By the late 1980s, only one in five marked it. Since then, the number has fallen to one in eight.[1]

There is a puzzling aspect to the decline. The percentage of college graduates in the population has tripled since 1960. Literacy tests, poll taxes, and lengthy residency requirements have been abolished. Registration has been simplified. Yet turnout has fallen.

What is going on here? Why are Americans less engaged by political campaigns today than even a few decades ago? Some analysts claim that participation follows a natural cycle and will therefore rise again, just as it did after downturns in the 1890s, 1920s, and 1940s. But this argument overlooks

This article has been adapted with permission of the publisher from *The Vanishing Voter,* by Thomas E. Patterson, Knopf, 2002.

the persistence of the current trend and the special nature of those earlier downturns (which were caused by the introduction of registration requirements, women's suffrage, and war weariness, respectively).

Analysts agree that generational replacement is part of the explanation for the decline. The civic-minded generations molded by the Depression and the Second World War have been gradually replaced by the more private-minded generation X and generation Y, who lived through childhood and adolescence without experiencing a grave crisis that called them to action. Today's young adults are less politically interested and informed than any cohort of young people on record. The voting rate of adults under age 30 was 50 percent in 1972. It barely exceeded 30 percent in 2000.

Generational replacement, however, is not the sole cause of the downward trend. Somehow, the United States has managed to create some of the least inviting and least savory campaigns imaginable. This development is the subject of this article, which is based on my recently published book *The Vanishing Voter*. The book, in turn, is an outgrowth of the Vanishing Voter Project, which was conducted during the 2000 campaign by the Joan Shorenstein Center on the Press, Politics, and Public Policy at Harvard University's Kennedy School of Government, with the support of a grant from the Pew Charitable Trusts. Our research team conducted weekly national surveys to discover why Americans were following or ignoring the campaign. By the time the study was concluded, we had interviewed nearly one hundred thousand Americans—easily the largest study of campaign involvement ever conducted (for information on the project, including state-by-state comparison of involvement level, see the project Website: www.vanishingvoter.org).

Competition, Anyone?

With party control of both the House and Senate at issue, the 2002 midterm election was a pundit's dream. However, the intense competition for control of Congress masked the fact that the vast majority of House races were uncompetitive. Only about three dozen of the 435 House seats were actually in play in 2002. In nearly twice that many districts, there was literally no serious competition: the weaker major party did not bother even to nominate a candidate. In several hundred other districts, the competition was so one-sided that the result was known even before the campaign began. As was the case in 2000, the victors won by an average margin of more than two to one.

House incumbents breezed to victory in 2002, just as they have in other recent election campaigns. Ninety-eight percent of the incumbents seeking another term in the House were reelected. U.S. House races are less competitive—and by a wide margin—than those of any other freely elected national legislative body in the world.

House incumbents have created a lock on the offices they hold. When the campaign finance laws were changed during the 1970s in reaction to Watergate, political action committees (PACs) suddenly sprouted, increasing in number from six hundred to four thousand within a decade. This new source of money turned out to be a bonanza for incumbents, since PACs are reluctant to oppose politicians who are already in power. Today, upwards of 85 percent of PAC money ends up in the pockets of incumbents,[2] who also operate year-around reelection campaigns at taxpayer expense. When members of Congress in the 1960s voted to greatly enlarge their personal staff, they argued that the additional personnel were needed to offset the executive branch's domination of policy information. However, an estimated 50 percent and more of congressional staff resources are devoted to public relations, constituency service, and other activities that serve primarily to keep House members in office.

Competition is the lifeblood of a democratic election, and when it dries up participation suffers. In many of the House districts in 2002, there was no campaign to speak of, and the news media provided little or no coverage. Voters in these districts were deprived of an opportunity to learn of the issues and the candidates and, on Election Day, to cast a meaningful vote. Analysts offer varying estimates of the effect of uncompetitive House races on turnout, but a 3–5 percent decrease is a reasonable figure.

Seated senators and governors find it harder to use their office in a way that ensures reelection, and these positions often attract challengers who are well heeled or well known. Close competition for these offices in a dozen states supplied excitement and interest to the 2002 election. The turnout average in these states was higher than it was in 1998. Yet competitive races have become an anomaly. The trend in House races is matched by what has been taking place in state legislatures. As these bodies have become more professionalized with larger staffs and salaries, their members have been able to use the advantages of being in office to stay in office and to turn politics into a lifelong career. In 2002, there were—continuing a trend—a record number of uncontested state legislative seats.

Many voters are also effectively disenfranchised by the way in which presidential primaries are structured. Front loading of the nominating schedule—the placement of a large number of state contests near the front end of the process—has led presidential hopefuls to raise and spend tens of millions on these early contests in an effort to secure nomination with a decisive victory on Super Tuesday. One effect is to make money the king of the nominating process. Not since John Connally in 1980 has the candidate who raised the most money before the first contests in Iowa and New Hampshire lost a nominating race.[3] A second effect is to deprive millions of citizens of the opportunity to cast a meaningful vote. Bush and Gore's Super Tuesday victories in 2000 completely devalued the yet-to-be-held presidential primaries and caucuses in other states. Turnout in those states was a third lower than that in the early-contest states and would have been next to nothing if nominations for other offices were not being contested. Our Vanishing Voter surveys revealed that residents of the late-scheduled states were also much less likely to talk about the campaign and to follow news about it. They were also less informed about the candidates and issues.

In the 1970s, when the nominating schedule unfolded a state at a time until the final month or so, the races lasted longer, money was less influential, and residents of nearly all states had a chance to cast a meaningful vote. Turnout nationally was twice the level that it is now.

In the presidential general election, Americans' opportunity to be part of the action is determined by the Electoral College. Although this feature of our constitutional system has always distorted the process to some extent, the fact that today's campaigns are based on money rather than volunteers has exaggerated the effect. Unlike volunteers, who work within the communities where they live, money can be targeted and withheld at will. During the 2000 general election campaign, there were no ad buys and no candidate visits in Kansas, a lopsidedly Republican state. In neighboring Missouri, which was a battleground state, there were eighteen candidate visits and millions of dollars were spent on televised political advertising. "The process effectively takes half the country and says, 'you're just spectators,'" notes Kathleen Hall Jamieson, dean of the University of Pennsylvania's Annenberg School of Communication.[4]

In 2000, residents of battleground states had a voting rate that was 3 percentage points higher than that of residents of other states. In fact, although the overall voting rate in 2000 was somewhat higher than it had been in 1996, turnout actually fell in nine states, all of which were safely in the Bush or Gore column. Residents of these and the other noncompetitive states also talked less about the campaign and paid less attention to election news than did the residents of battleground states.[5]

Clear-Cut Parties, Anyone?

The issue of whether voters have a choice includes the clarity and significance of that choice. Here, too, the situation is less favorable than it once was.

There was a long period in American history when elections were waged on economic issues powerful enough to define the two major parties and divide the public. These issues stemmed from Americans' deepest hopes and fears and had the power to cement their loyalty to a party and draw them to the polls. That era ended with the triumph of Franklin Roosevelt's New Deal, which (along with Lyndon Johnson's Great Society) put in place government programs that greatly reduced the sources of economic resentment and insecurity that had fueled party conflict. A safety net for the economically vulnerable was in place, as were policy mechanisms for stabilizing the economy. An electoral majority that could be easily rallied by calls for economic redistribution no longer existed.

As the impact of economic issues on voting behavior weakened, a large set of less comprehensive issues emerged. Civil rights, street crime, school prayer, and welfare dependency were among the earliest of these issues, which were followed by abortion, the environment, education, global trade, and others. All were important, but they intersected with each other in confounding ways.

None had the reach or the endurance of the economic issues. As a result, the issues of one election were usually different from the issues that had dominated the previous election or would be at the forefront in the next one.

How could the political parties create cohesive and enduring coalitions out of this mix of issues? The short answer is that they could not do so. The issues were too crosscutting and too numerous for either party to combine them in a way that could easily satisfy a following. By the 1970s, self-described independents accounted for a third of the electorate. People also found it increasingly difficult to think and talk about the parties. Americans were better educated than they had been in the 1950s, but they had a harder time saying what the parties represented. In the 1950s, fewer than one in ten had nothing to say when asked in polls what they liked and disliked about the parties. By the 1970s, three in ten had nothing to say.[6]

Since then, political parties have not recovered their prominence. The two major parties are now relatively weak objects of loyalty and thought, and the decline in party loyalty and identification has diminished Americans' concern with election politics. Like any other emotional attachment, party loyalty heightens interest and commitment. For its part, party awareness reflects people's ability to recognize what is at stake in election politics and the options available to them.[7] "My mind has just gone blank," said a Florida resident in 2000 when asked in one of our surveys to describe the parties.[8]

Americans who today have a party loyalty and awareness of the parties have a voting rate more than twice that of those who call themselves independent and who cannot find words with which to describe the parties. This was true also in the 1950s; the difference today is that the percentage of citizens in the high-voting group is much smaller and the percentage in the low-voting group is much larger than in the 1950s.[9] The type of citizen who votes less often has been gradually replacing the type who votes more often.

The change in party politics helps to explain why, disproportionately, the decline in participation has been concentrated among Americans of low income. Although a class bias in turnout has been a persistent feature of U.S. elections, the gap has now widened to a chasm. The voting rate among those at the bottom of the income ladder is only half that of those at the top. During the era when the electorate was divided by basic economic issues, working-class Americans were at the center of political debate and party conflict. They now occupy the periphery of a political world in which money and middle-class concerns are ascendant. In 2000, low-income respondents were roughly 30 percent more likely than those in the middle or top income groups to say the election's outcome would have little or no impact on their lives.[10]

The change in party politics also helps to explain why candidates now have trouble crafting a message that voters find compelling. Candidates have never had so many communication weapons at their disposal, yet they have never found it so hard to frame their message. As Franklin Roosevelt's voice crackled into living rooms through the vacuum-tube radio, his pledge to "the forgotten man" had a persuasive power that today's media consultants would envy. Listeners didn't have to be told what FDR had in mind or to whom he was speaking. Campaign messages today are strikingly different in the range of issues they address, the contradictions they contain, the speed with which they turn over, and the small percentage of voters with whom they resonate. After their defeat in the 2002 midterm election, Democratic leaders were roundly criticized for failing to put out a message that captivated voters. However, Democratic politicians are neither stupid nor apolitical. If a simple and compelling message were readily available, they would have seized it. Such messages are today quite rare. If Republicans could not rely on their perennial "let's cut taxes" pitch—which is now closer to a fight song than a true governing philosophy—they would face the same problem.

A century ago, James Bryce worried that the growing complexity of American society threatened the parties' ability to forge and mobilize a cohesive majority. Social complexity is now orders of magnitude greater and has clearly overtaken the parties. The consequences include a lower rate of electoral participation.

Uplifting Campaigns, Anyone?

Beginning in the late 1950s and early 1960s, control of an election campaign began to shift from the political parties to the candidates, largely because of television and refinement in techniques of mass persuasion. Americans were initially thrilled by the chance for a close-up look at the candidates and their campaigns. Theodore H. White's *The Making of the President, 1960*, topped the best-seller list.

However, Americans have come to dislike nearly everything about the modern campaign. The new style has brought out aspects of politics that were once largely out of sight. Ambition, manipulation, and deception have become as prominent as issues of policy and leadership. But politicking, like sausage making, is best viewed from a distance. An election is supposed to bring out the issues. It is not supposed to ruin one's appetite, but that's the best way to understand much of what Americans now see during a campaign and why they don't have much taste for it.

Negative campaigning has long been part of campaign politics but now dominates it. Candidates have discovered that it is easier in many situations to attract swing voters by tearing down one's opponent than by talking about one's own platform. Research indicates that negative advertising has more than tripled since the 1960s. Such ads now account for well over half the ads featured in most presidential and congressional races.[11]

Our surveys indicate that a cumulative effect of negative politics, campaign after campaign, is reduced interest in the election. Attack politics wears some people down to the point where they simply don't want to hear about the campaign. On an average day during the 2000 campaign, Americans who believed that negative messages are a defining feature of U.S. elections were less likely than those who had a different view of the prominence of such messages to discuss the campaign and pay attention to news about it. The difference was not large, but it occurred across the course of the campaign. Day in and day out, those who believed campaigns are akin to mud wrestling were less attentive to the campaign, even when level of education and income were controlled.[12]

Today's campaigns are also characterized by promises—endless promises. Unlike their predecessors in the age of party-centered politics, today's candidates are unable to campaign on broad statements of principle within the context of a reliable base of party loyalists. Today's candidates build their following by pledges of support to nearly every conceivable voting group. The changing nature of party platforms tells the story. Whereas the platform was once a declaration of broad goals and ideals, it has become a promissory note to special interests. The 1948 Democratic and Republican platforms were less than three thousand words in length. By the 1980s, they exceeded twenty thousand words.[13]

An effect of this relentless flow of campaign promises is a public wary of taking candidates at their word. In our Vanishing Voter surveys during the 2000 campaign, 81 percent agreed with the statement "most politicians will say almost anything to get themselves elected." Respondents who felt this way had a significantly lower voting rate than others; they were also less likely to talk about the campaign and follow news about it.

Modern-day politics also exalts personality, increasing the likelihood that personal blunders and failings will loom large in a campaign. Through the 1972 presidential election, personal controversy did not receive even half as much news coverage as did policy issues. Since 1972, it has received nearly equal time.[14] Even a short list indicates just how salient personal controversy has become: Gerald Ford's blundering statement on Eastern Europe, Jimmy Carter's "lust in my heart" *Playboy* interview, Geraldine Ferraro's tax returns, Gary Hart's affair with Donna Rice, Dan Quayle's assault on the fictional Murphy Brown, Bill Clinton's relationship with Gennifer Flowers, and Al Gore's Buddhist Temple appearance. The revelation in 2000 that Bush had been arrested a quarter century earlier for drunken driving dominated the headlines in the closing days of the campaign. The incident got more coverage on the evening newscasts in a few days than did all of Bush and Gore's foreign policy statements during the entire general election.[15]

Although a startling revelation can perk up a campaign, citizens do not particularly like the prominence it attains. In our surveys, 62 percent agreed with the statement "political campaigns today seem more like theater or entertainment than something to be taken seriously." Although those who held this opinion were no less likely than others to vote on Election Day, they were less likely to discuss election politics and to attend to news about it.

The length of the modern campaign is also a turnoff for many Americans. Today's candidates are self-starters who depend on themselves rather than the party to win nomination and election. As a result, active campaigning now begins much earlier in the election year than it once did. In our 2000 election surveys, respondents repeatedly expressed displeasure with the campaign's length. The long campaign also numbed people to the point where many tuned it out. A week before the 2000 Republican national convention, only one in five American respondents knew it was only days away. Not surprisingly, a large share of those who ended up watching the Republican convention did so only because they stumbled across it while channel surfing.

Americans' disenchantment with campaigns is not the major reason for their declining participation rate, but it is one of them. Unsavory campaigns also leave a sour taste even with those who do vote. In the concluding week of the 2000 campaign, when asked whether the campaign had been "rather depressing, that it hasn't been nearly as good as a campaign should be" or whether it had been "uplifting, that it made [you] feel better about elections," respondents in our survey said by more than two to one that the campaign had been depressing.

Good News, Anyone?

On the network evening newscasts during the 2000 general election, George W. Bush's coverage was 63 percent negative in tone and only 37 percent positive. Al Gore's coverage was no better. A good deal of Bush's coverage suggested that he was not too smart. There were nine such claims in the news for every contrary claim. Gore's coverage was dotted with suggestions he was not all that truthful. Such claims outpaced rebuttals by seventeen to one.[16]

Although the press is often accused of having a liberal bias, its real bias is a preference for the negative. The news was not always so downbeat. When John F. Kennedy and Richard Nixon sought the presidency in 1960, 75 percent of their coverage was favorable in tone and only 25 percent was unfavorable. By the 1980s campaign, however, election news coverage had reached a point where more than half of it was negative. Since then, no major-party presidential nominee has received on balance more positive news than negative news.[17]

This change is attributable in part to the poisonous effect of Vietnam and Watergate on the relationship between the journalist and the politician. A larger influence, however, has been the emergence of an interpretive style of reporting. In the 1960s, this style began to supplant the older descriptive style in which the journalist's main goal was straightforward reporting of the facts of events. Since the facts were often based on what newsmakers had said or done, they had considerable control over the coverage they received. Much of the "good press" that Kennedy and Nixon received in 1960 came from what they themselves said about their candidacy.

On the other hand, interpretive journalism thrusts the reporter into the role of analyst and judge. The journalist gives meaning to a news event by supplying the analytical context. The journalist is thus positioned to give shape to the news in a way that the descriptive style did not allow. The power of the journalist to construct the news is apparent from the extent to which journalistic voices now dominate the coverage. Whereas reporters were once the passive voice behind the news, they now get more time than the newsmakers they cover. On the nightly newscasts, the journalists covering Bush and Gore in 2000 spoke six minutes for every minute the candidates spoke.[18]

Interpretive reporting has unleashed the skepticism traditional in American journalism. The candidates' failings and disputes have been played up; their successes and overtures have been played down. The 1996 Republican nominating race is a case in point. Media analyst Robert Lichter examined the GOP hopefuls' television ads and stump speeches. Over half the ads (56 percent) were positive in tone and nearly two-thirds (66 percent) of the assertions in candidate speeches were positive statements about what they hoped to accomplish if elected. These dimensions of the Republican campaign were seldom mentioned in news reports. The candidates' negative ads and their attacks on opponents filled the news. "Forget about the issues," ABC's Peter Jennings said of the Republican race, "there is enough mud being tossed around . . . to keep a health spa supplied for a lifetime."[19]

The tone of news coverage affects people's opinions about candidates. A study of the 1960–1992 campaigns found that a negative impression of presidential candidates increased step by step with the increase in negative coverage.[20] Gallup polls are another indicator of the effect of the increase in negative coverage. Between 1936 and 1968, Barry Goldwater was the only major-party presidential nominee whose public image at the end of the campaign was more negative than positive. Since 1968, in the era of interpretive journalism, a third of the presidential nominees have been perceived unfavorably and another third have had marginally favorable ratings.

Negative news is only one of the reasons Americans are dissatisfied with candidates and campaigns, but it is clearly among those reasons.

What Might Be Done to Reverse the Trend?

The developments that have diminished Americans' interest in election politics are deep rooted and unlikely to be reversed easily or soon. Campaign participation in all its forms, from voting to watching debates, could continue its downward slide.

There are some changes that would retard the trend. Election Day registration is one of them. In the 1950s, 90 percent of Americans lived in a state that closed its registration rolls two or more weeks in advance of the election.[21] The situation is not much different now; today, 87 percent live in a state that shuts down registration two or more weeks before Election Day.[22] In the six states that allow Election Day registration, turnout in 2000 was 15 percentage points higher than elsewhere. Although these states (which include

Minnesota and Wisconsin) have a history of a high participation rate, all of them moved up in the turnout rankings after implementing same-day registration. Studies indicate that universal same-day registration could boost turnout by as much as 5 percentage points.[23]

Turnout would also increase if polling hours were extended. Amid the uproar over ballot irregularities in Florida in 2000, no commentator saw fit to ask why the polls in that state close at 7:00 P.M. local time. Florida is one of twenty-six states that shut down their polls before 8:00 P.M. Not surprisingly, turnout in these states is several percentage points below that of states where the polls are open until 8:00 P.M. or later. Limits on polling hours go back decades and have been a convenient way to discourage the participation of lower-income workers, who are stuck at their jobs during the day and do not get home in time to cast a ballot.

Turnout might also increase if Election Day were declared a national holiday, as the National Commission on Federal Election Reform has recommended. It is noteworthy that support for this reform, as well as for same-day registration and extended polling hours, is highest among young adults. They are particularly likely to forget to register on time and to require an extra boost to get them to the polls on Election Day. They would benefit most from laws that make participation easier.[24]

Structural change by itself will not be enough to turn things around. When turnout dropped sharply in the 1920s, Arthur M. Schlesinger and Erik McKinley Eriksson wrote "no stone should be left unturned" in the effort to lure citizens back to the polls.[25] Today, the schools can do more to give students a decent civic education and help them register so that the first election upon graduation is a step toward lifelong participation. Other entities—the churches, news media, universities, nonprofits, unions, and corporations—must also use their power to assist people in exercising the vote, because if citizens cannot be encouraged to participate more fully the nation will face the far greater challenge of how to maintain self-government when people don't vote.

Notes

1. Federal Elections Commission data.

2. Federal Elections Commission data.

3. Norrander, B. "Candidate Attrition During the Presidential Nominating System." Paper presented at the Joan Shorenstein Center on the Press, Politics, and Public Policy roundtable, John F. Kennedy School of Government, Harvard University, Oct. 16, 2000.

4. Quoted in Marks, P. "The Forgotten State: Dearth of Ads Makes Race in Kansas a Snooze." New York Times, Oct. 27, 2000, p. A26.

5. Vanishing Voter Survey data.

6. National Election Studies data.

7. See Wattenberg, M. P. The Decline of American Political Parties, 1952–1996. Cambridge, Mass.: Harvard University Press, 1998.

8. Vanishing Voter Survey, Nov. 3–7, 2000.

9. National Election Studies data, 1952–2000.

10. The question was asked in several surveys. Across all of them, 46 percent of those in the bottom third, compared with 36 percent in the middle third and 32 percent in the upper third, said the election's outcome would have little or no effect on their lives.

11. See, for example, West, D. M. *Air Wars: Television Advertising in Election Campaigns, 1952–1992.* Washington, D.C.: Congressional Quarterly Press, 1993.

12. Vanishing Voter survey data.

13. Fishel, J. *Presidents and Promises: From Campaign Pledge to Presidential Performance.* Washington, D.C.: Congressional Quarterly Press, 1985.

14. Patterson, T. E. *Out of Order.* New York: Knopf, 1993, chapter four.

15. Patterson, T. E. *The Vanishing Voter.* New York: Knopf, 2002.

16. See Lichter, R. "A Plague on Both Your Parties: Substance and Fairness in TV Election News." *Harvard International Journal of Press/Politics,* 2001, 6(6), 16; Project for Excellence in Journalism data, Web download Mar. 7, 2002.

17. Patterson (1993), chapter one.

18. Lichter (2001).

19. "The Bad News Campaign." *Media Monitor,* 1996, 10(2), 3–6.

20. Patterson (1993), chapter one.

21. Rosenstone, S. J., and Hansen, J. M. *Mobilization, Participation, and Democracy in America.* New York: Macmillan, 1993.

22. Percentage calculated from Federal Election Commission data.

23. Fenster, M. J. "The Impact of Allowing Day of Registration Voting on Turnout in the United States from 1960 to 1992." *American Politics Quarterly,* 1994, 22, 74–87.

24. Patterson (2002), chapter six.

25. Schlesinger, A. M., and Eriksson, E. M. "The Vanishing Voter." *New Republic,* Oct. 15, 1924, p. 147. The rest of this paragraph and the article's final sentence are indebted to the final paragraph of their article, even to the choice of the phrasing and some of the words in the final sentence.

Thomas E. Patterson is Bradlee Professor of Government and the Press at Harvard University's Kennedy School of Government.

Healthy Municipalities: Now, "It's the Only Way to Go!"

Leonard J. Duhl, M.D.

For most of my professional lifetime I have been preoccupied with the fact that medical care accounts for only 10 percent of what contributes to health. Indeed, medicine is affected by factors outside the fields of direct medical care. It was for this reason that I became concerned with community.

Community encompasses many things and can be defined in many ways. One of the most important issues is how community affects individuals' and institutions' ability to deal with life problems. These abilities require personal and social capital. The concept underlying Healthy Cities focuses on building personal and social capital, but the Healthy Cities movement is not a program or project in the conventional sense. Rather, it is a set of individualized processes for communities and people to learn how to improve their quality of life.

In trying to articulate a more encompassing sense of what we mean by health, we have used the words *health for all, primary health care, health promotion,* and *healthy public policy* to broaden our scope of concern. These concepts have stood for creating complex systems that increase access to health care resources, create equity in their distribution, and promote people's active participation in making decisions about their own health. It is not difficult to present figures showing great inequity in human rights, ownership of capital by the poor;[1] health resources; usable income; and the incidence of AIDS, diarrheal disease, and depression. In all these cases and others, we need increasing awareness of the complex interacting systems and the variety of players involved in both promoting well-being and entering the disease cycle early and effectively.

When I began my work with broad participatory community systems and health, these ideas were rejected by the highest of medical authorities, in my own country and others and in WHO and UNICEF. Fortunately, some are now

This article was adapted from the Abraham Horwitz Award lecture delivered by Leonard J. Duhl, M.D., on September 25, 2002, at the Pan American Health Organization, Washington, D.C.

saying, "It's the only way to go!"[2] I quote the United Nations Development Programme's *Development Report, 2002*: "Politics matter for human development. Reducing poverty depends as much on whether poor people have political power as on their opportunities for economic progress. Democracy has proven to be the system of governance most capable of mediating and preventing conflict and of securing and sustaining well-being. By expanding people's choices about how and by whom they are governed, democracy brings principles of participation and accountability to the process of human development."[3]

Through the work of the Pan American Health Organization (PAHO), and especially during the time Abraham Horwitz was its director (1958–1975), much was accomplished in disease reduction in Latin America. In more recent years, there has been a greater focus on political and social infrastructure. However, the impact of these advances has been limited by the process of historical forgetting, which has affected both the indigenous cultures that preceded the arrival of Western Europeans and the Western cultures that took root in Latin America. Pre-Columbian societies possessed a great sense of community, independence, and competence as well as notable skills of government and science. The societies that developed after the arrival of the conquistadors forgot the emphasis on relationships, caring, and community that were a hallmark of the early writings of the Judeo-Christian tradition. If these two traditions had meshed, the tumultuous history of Latin America would have been different. Community could have been the core value of society.

As the history of Latin America unfolded, a vast separation developed between the conquerors and the conquered, with great benefits flowing to the former. Whether it was gold or, more contemporarily, economic profits, this outflow from communities left them increasingly fragmented and created many so-called superfluous people. Dictatorship of all kinds flourished, and the gap between rich and poor grew. Leadership came from the "haves." Corruption became widespread. The poor in the rural areas began to migrate to the *favellas* in the cities, which continue to grow almost unfettered.

A sense of community was missing. Whether this sense derived from indigenous values or from those of early Catholic traditions, the actual communities that developed became fragmented and separate worlds where greed dominated and the poor were left to fend for themselves. Today we see innumerable children living a shortened life on the streets amid a lack of health services and education. Poverty is pervasive, and hope is dying. If hope dies, people grow apathetic. But if even a spark of hope is still present, people strike out and try mightily to find a better life. All too often, though, they reach for new sources of strength—through violence, guns, and drugs. We also see WHO reports of eight hundred million depressed people worldwide. The economic policies of my country, and those of the IMF and World Bank, have not helped this situation.

We must turn to health promotion, not just treatment. The Ottawa Charter for Health Promotion, in which all the countries in the Americas participated, presents these words:

> Health promotion is the process of enabling people to increase control over, and to improve, their health. To reach a state of complete physical, mental and social well-being, an individual or group must be able to identify and to realize aspirations, to satisfy needs, and to change or cope with the environment. Health is, therefore, seen as a resource for everyday life, not the objective of living. Health is a positive concept emphasizing social and personal resources, as well as physical capacities. Therefore, health promotion is not just the responsibility of the health sector but goes beyond healthy lifestyles to well-being.[4]

The essence of this belief is community. To get there we need a new paradigm of health. What are the elements of this paradigm?

- A broad definition of health
- A broad definition of community
- A shared vision based on community values
- Improved quality of life for everyone
- Diverse citizen participation and widespread community ownership
- Focus on systems change
- Development of local assets and resources
- Benchmarks and measures of progress and outcome

The elements of a healthy city/community include

- A sense of history, shared by citizens, upon which their commonly held values are based
- Multidimensionality and a complex interactive economy
- A striving for decentralization of power and citizen participation in making decisions about policy
- Representation that focuses on the whole of a city or community and can visualize both the parts and the whole simultaneously
- The ability to adapt to change, cope with breakdown, and learn from their own experiences and those of other cities and communities
- The support and maintenance of infrastructures

Comprehensive intersectoral initiatives in other related areas of concern, such as environmental sustainability, transportation, safety, education, antidrug programs, and urban planning, are connected by certain underlying values, among them the active participation of multiple community groups, institutions, and citizens to resolve conflict and create and carry out a plan. In such a process, there is awareness of reciprocity—what was called reciprocal maintenance in the Ottawa Charter—and the importance of being able to trust others, which facilitates cooperation for mutual benefit. For all these processes, there is a need to build and create both personal and social capital.

To build social capital requires social entrepreneurs[5] who (with all the skill of business entrepreneurs) can organize, manage, teach, and lead social programs. Interestingly, most of the social entrepreneurs worldwide are women. Could it be they understand complex systems better than their male counterparts do?

The Healthy Cities/Healthy Communities movement has found that the focal point of organizing and building social capital can be any of a number of issues, including urbanization, environmental disaster, economic development and capital-building efforts,[6] health promotion, health care system reform, sustainable environments, and especially the problems of youth.

In connection with this last point, I want to underscore the importance of mentoring youth and creating leadership for the future. In my work with a seventy-two-year-old camp called Rising Sun,[7] we have brought boys and girls age thirteen to sixteen from throughout the world—many from Latin America—who probably would not make it without this boost, and helped to give them the mentoring they need for a better life. We have seen many of these young people later assume key leadership positions throughout the world. What better activity for PAHO than planning for the future through improving the life chances for young people?

Communities throughout Latin America are at the beginning of a profound transition as they take up such issues as environmental awareness, community participation, and concern for human rights. PAHO has played a key role in facilitating discussion on these issues. We as a species have a moral, economic, and ecological responsibility to ensure the continuation of this process into the next century.

Notes

1. "Capital is the force that raises the productivity of labor and creates the wealth of nations. It is the lifeblood of the capitalist system, the foundation of progress, and the one thing that the poor countries of the world cannot seem to produce for themselves, no matter how eagerly their people engage in all the other activities that characterize a capitalist economy." De Soto, H. *The Mystery of Capital.* New York: Basic Books, 2000. Quoted in review by Dan Blatt in *Futurecasts* online magazine, 4(8), accessed Aug. 1, 2002. (http://www.futurecasts.com/book%20review%2026.htm)

2. In introducing me recently, Philip Lee, M.D. (former assistant secretary for health in HEW and HHS), said, "When Len told me about these ideas forty years ago, I told him they were irrelevant. Now, it's the only way to go!"

3. United Nations Development Programme. *Development Report, 2002.* (http://www.undp.org/hdr2002/)

4. *Ottawa Charter for Health Promotion,* First International Conference on Health Promotion, Ottawa, Canada, Nov. 21, 1986.

5. Duhl, L. *The Social Entrepreneurship of Change.* Putnam Valley, N.Y.: Cogent Press, 2000.

6. Duhl (2000). De Soto (2000) notes that many Latin American nations have tried capitalism on four separate occasions during the last two centuries and failed all four times. Numerous market weaknesses or lack of budgetary and monetary discipline played a major role in all of these failures. The degree of defectiveness is highlighted by the fact that perfection is not required for prosperity—and that it is far from achieved even in the advanced nations.

7. See http://www.risingsun.org.

Leonard J. Duhl, M.D., is professor of public health and urban planning at the University of California, Berkeley.

ORDERING INFORMATION

National Civic League Council of Advisors

National Civic League Publications List

ALL PRICES include shipping and handling (for orders outside the United States, please add $15 for shipping). National Civic League members receive a 10 percent discount. Bulk rates are available. See end of this list for ordering information.

Most Frequently Requested Publications

The Civic Index: A New Approach to Improving Community Life
National Civic League staff, 1993
50 pp., 7 × 10 paper, $7.00

The Community Visioning and Strategic Planning Handbook
National Civic League staff, 1995
53 pp., $23.00

Governance

National Report on Local Campaign Finance Reform
New Politics Program staff, 1998
96 pp., $15.00

Communities and the Voting Rights Act
National Civic League staff, 1996
118 pp., 8.5 × 11 paper, $12.00

Forms of Local Government
National Civic League staff, 1993
15 pp., 5.5 × 8.5 pamphlet, $3.00

Guide for Charter Commissions (Fifth Edition)
National Civic League staff, 1991
46 pp., 6 × 9 paper, $10.00

Handbook for Council Members in Council-Manager Cities (Fifth Edition)
National Civic League staff, 1992
38 pp., 6 × 9 paper, $12.00

Measuring City Hall Performance: Finally, A How-To Guide
Charles K. Bens, 1991
127 pp., 8.5 × 11 monograph, $15.00

Model County Charter (Revised Edition)
National Civic League staff, 1990
53 pp., 5.5 × 8.5 paper, $10.00

Modern Counties: Professional Management—The Non-Charter Route
National Civic League staff, 1993
54 pp., paper, $8.00

Term Limitations for Local Officials: A Citizen's Guide to Constructive Dialogue
Laurie Hirschfeld Zeller, 1992
24 pp., 5.5 × 8.5 pamphlet, $3.00

Using Performance Measurement in Local Government: A Guide to Improving Decisions, Performance, and Accountability
Paul D. Epstein, 1988
225 pp., 6 × 9 paper, $5.00

Model City Charter (Seventh Edition)
National Civic League staff, 1997
110 pp., 5.5 × 8.5 monograph, $14.00

Alliance for National Renewal

ANR Community Resource Manual
National Civic League Staff, 1996
80 pp., 8.5 × 11, $6.00

Taking Action: Building Communities That Strengthen Families
Special section in *Governing Magazine,* 1998
8 pp., 8.5 × 11 (color), $3.00

Communities That Strengthen Families
Insert in *Governing Magazine,* 1997
8 pp., 8.5 × 11 reprint, $3.00

Connecting Government and Neighborhoods
Insert in *Governing Magazine,* 1996
8 pp., 8.5 × 11 reprint, $3.00

The Culture of Renewal
Richard Louv, 1996
45 pp., $8.00

The Kitchen Table
Quarterly newsletter of Alliance for National Renewal, 1999
8 pp., annual subscription (4 issues) $12.00, free to ANR Partners

The Landscape of Civic Renewal
Civic renewal projects and studies from around the country, 1999
185 pp., $12.00

National Renewal
John W. Gardner, 1995
27 pp., 7 × 10, $7.00

San Francisco Civic Scan
Richard Louv, 1996
100 pp., $6.00

1998 Guide to the Alliance for National Renewal
National Civic League staff, 1998
50 pp., 4 × 9, $5.00

Springfield, Missouri: A Nice Community Wrestles with How to Become a Good Community
Alliance for National Renewal staff, 1996
13 pp., $7.00

Toward a Paradigm of Community-Making
Allan Wallis, 1996
60 pp., $12.00

The We Decade: Rebirth on Community
Dallas Morning News, 1995
39 pp., 8.5 × 14 reprint, $3.00

99 Things You Can Do for Your Community in 1999
poster (folded), $6.00

Healthy Communities

Healthy Communities Handbook
National Civic League staff, 1993
162 pp., 8.5 × 11 monograph, $22.00

All-America City Awards

All-America City Yearbook (1991, 1992, 1993, 1994, 1995, 1996, 1997)
National Civic League staff
60 pp., 7 × 10 paper, $4.00 shipping and handling

All-America City Awards Audio Tape Briefing
Audiotape, $4.00 shipping and handling

Diversity and Regionalism

Governance and Diversity:
Findings from Oakland, 1995
Findings from Fresno, 1995
Findings from Los Angeles, 1994
National Civic League staff
7 × 10 paper, $5.00 each

Networks, Trust and Values
Allan D. Wallis, 1994
51 pp., 7 × 10 paper, $7.00

Inventing Regionalism
Allan D. Wallis, 1995
75 pp., 8.5 × 11 monograph, $19.00

Leadership, Collaboration, and Community Building

Citistates: How Urban America Can Prosper in a Competitive World
Neal Peirce, Curtis Johnson, and John Stuart Hall, 1993
359 pp., 6.5 × 9.5, $25.00

Collaborative Leadership
David D. Chrislip and Carl E. Larson, 1994
192 pp., 6 × 9.5, $20.00

Good City and the Good Life
Daniel Kemmis, 1995
226 pp., 6 × 8.5, $23.00

On Leadership
John W. Gardner, 1990
220 pp., 6 × 9.5, $28.00

Politics for People: Finding a Responsible Public Voice
David Mathews, 1994
229 pp., 6 × 9.5, $20.00

Public Journalism and Public Life
David "Buzz" Merritt, 1994
129 pp., 6 × 9, $30.00

Resolving Municipal Disputes
David Stiebel, 1992
2 audiotapes and book, $15.00

Time Present, Time Past
Bill Bradley, former chairman of the National Civic League, 1996
450 pp., paper, $13.00

Transforming Politics
David D. Chrislip, 1995
12 pp., 7 × 10, $3.00

Revolution of the Heart
Bill Shore, 1996
167 pp., 8.5 × 5.75, $8.00

The Web of Life
Richard Louv, 1996
258 pp., 7.5 × 5.5, $15.00

Programs for Community Problem Solving

Systems Reform and Local Government: Improving Outcomes for Children, Families, and Neighborhoods
1998, 47 pp., $12.00

Building Community: Exploring the Role of Social Capital and Local Government
1998, 31 pp., $12.00

The Transformative Power of Governance: Strengthening Community Capacity to Improve Outcomes for Children, Families, and Neighborhoods
1998, 33 pp., $12.00

Building the Collaborative Community
Jointly published by the National Civic League and the National Institute for Dispute Resolution, 1994
33 pp., $12.00

Negotiated Approaches to Environmental Decision Making in Communities: An Exploration of Lessons Learned
Jointly published by the National Institute for Dispute Resolution and the Coalition to Improve Management in State and Local Government, 1996
58 pp., $14.00

Community Problem Solving Case Summaries, Volume III
1992, 52 pp., $19.00

Facing Racial and Cultural Conflicts: Tools for Rebuilding Community (Second Edition)
1994, $24.00

Collaborative Transportation Planning Guidelines for Implementing ISTEA and the CAAA
1993, 87 pp., $14.00

Collaborative Planning Video
Produced by the American Planning Association, 1995
6-hr. video and 46 pp. workshop materials, $103.00

Pulling Together: A Land Use and Development Consensus Building Manual
A joint publication of PCPS and the Urban Land Institute, 1994
145 pp., $34.00

Solving Community Problems by Consensus
1990, 20 pp., $14.00

Involving Citizens in Community Decision Making: A Guidebook
1992, 30 pp., $30.00

NATIONAL CIVIC LEAGUE sales policies: Orders must be paid in advance by check, VISA, or MasterCard. We are unable to process exchanges, returns, credits, or refunds. For orders outside the United States, add $15 for shipping.

TO PLACE AN ORDER:

CALL the National Civic League at (303) 571–4343 or (800) 223–6004, or

MAIL ORDERS TO:
National Civic League
1445 Market Street, Suite 300
Denver, CO 80202–1717, or

E-MAIL the National Civic League at ncl@ncl.org